Student Study Guide to accompany

exploring the dimensions of

Human Sexuality

third edition

Stephanie M. Chisolm, PhD
James Madison University

JONES AND BARTLETT PUBLISHERS
Sudbury, Massachusetts
BOSTON   TORONTO   LONDON   SINGAPORE

World Headquarters

Jones and Bartlett Publishers
40 Tall Pine Drive
Sudbury, MA 01776
978-443-5000
info@jbpub.com
www.jbpub.com

Jones and Bartlett Publishers Canada
6339 Ormindale Way
Mississauga, ON L5V 1J2
CANADA

Jones and Bartlett Publishers International
Barb House, Barb Mews
London W6 7PA
UK

Jones and Bartlett's books and products are available through most bookstores and online booksellers. To contact Jones and Bartlett Publishers directly, call 800-832-0034, fax 978-443-8000, or visit our web site, www.jbpub.com.

Substantial discounts on bulk quantities of Jones and Bartlett's publications are available to corporations, professional associations, and other qualified organizations. For details and specific discount information, contact the special sales department at Jones and Bartlett via the above contact information or send an e-mail to specialsales@jbpub.com.

Production Credits

V.P., Manufacturing and Inventory Control: Therese Connell
Acquisitions Editor: Jacqueline Mark-Geraci
Production Editor: Susan Schultz
Editorial Assistant: Amy Flagg
Associate Marketing Manager: Wendy Thayer
Interior and Cover Design: Anne Spencer
Composition: Shepherd, Inc.
Cover Image: © Image Source/Alamy
Printing and Binding: Courier Corporation

6048

Printed in the United States of America
11 10 09 08 07 06   10 9 8 7 6 5 4 3 2 1

Contents

Introduction v
Note-Taking Tips vii
Chapter 1: Introducing the Dimensions of Human Sexuality 1
Chapter 2: Sexuality Research 15
Chapter 3: Sexual Communication 32
Chapter 4: Female Sexual Anatomy and Physiology 48
Chapter 5: Male Sexual Anatomy and Physiology 65
In Focus: Body Image 78
Chapter 6: Gender Dimensions 82
Chapter 7: Sexual Response and Arousal 93
Chapter 8: Contraception 107
Chapter 9: Conception, Pregnancy, and Birth 123
In Focus: Unexpected Pregnancy Outcomes 141
Chapter 10: Sexual Techniques and Behavior 146
Chapter 11: Sexual Orientation 157
Chapter 12: Sexuality in Childhood and Adolescence 168
Chapter 13: Sexuality in Adulthood 182
Chapter 14: Sexually Transmitted Infections 196
In Focus: HIV and AIDS 212
Chapter 15: Sexual Dysfunction and Therapy 217
In Focus: Atypical Sexual Behaviors 232
Chapter 16: Forcible Sexual Behaviors 236
Chapter 17: Sexual Consumerism 251
Chapter 18: Sexual Ethics, Morality, and the Law 265

Introduction

Human sexuality is important and complex enough to study for an entire semester. For some students this course is required to fulfill degree requirements for graduation; others choose this as an elective. Most students are surprised at the volume of information covered in a course in human sexuality, and sometimes do not appreciate the multiple dimensions and body of knowledge until after the first quiz or exam.

Each of us brings unique backgrounds, experiences, values, and beliefs to discussions of human sexuality issues. These factors influence your sexuality and sexual decision making in a variety of ways.

In this course and text, you will learn that each of us is a sexual being, regardless of whether we choose to act on our sexuality or not. This may well be the most personally useful course you take in your academic career. The knowledge gained in this course can both protect and enhance your life.

This Study Guide is designed to help you organize and reinforce your learning about the sexuality issues covered in *Exploring the Dimensions of Human Sexuality, Third Edition*. The following features can be found in most of the chapters:

- **Learning Objectives**   Give you an idea of what you are expected to know after reading each chapter of the text.

- **Lecture Slides**   Help you to have organized notes, which is essential at exam time and when doing assignments.

- **Chapter Summary: Fill in the Blanks**   Test and refresh your memory on the topics covered in each chapter.

- **Focus on the Facts**   Organize your review of the sexuality-related research topics or studies found in each chapter.

- **Activities**   Apply or practice what you learn in class, and in your text.

- **Web-EX**   Explore key concepts in human sexuality with these Internet-based learning exercises.

- **True/False, Matching, and Other Self-tests.**

Lecture Slides

The lecture slide component is located directly after the learning objectives in each chapter and contains the full set of PowerPoint slides that accompany your textbook as well as space next to each slide for you to jot down the terms and concepts that you feel are most important to each lecture. This guide will save you from having to write down everything that is on the slides. Do the assigned reading, listen in lecture, follow the key points your instructor makes, and write down meaningful notes. This is the perfect place to write down questions that you want to ask your professor later or reminders to yourself to go back and study a certain concept again to make sure you really got it.

For more information on the most effective note-taking methods that will save you both time and effort when reviewing for exams, see the section on Note-Taking Tips directly following this Introduction.

Once the lecture slides component of this Study Guide has helped to organize and simplify your notes on each chapter, the exercises and assessments in the remaining sections will test how well you have mastered the material. Your ability to easily locate the important concepts of a recent lecture and test yourself on the most important points and terminology will prove to be essential at exam time.

This Study Guide is a valuable resource. You've found a wonderful study partner!

Note-Taking Tips

1. It is easier to take notes if you are not hearing the information for the first time. Read the chapter or the material that is about to be discussed before class. This will help you to anticipate what will be said in class and have an idea of what to write down. It will also help to read over your notes from the previous class. This way you can avoid having to spend the first few minutes of class trying to remember where you left off last time.

2. Don't waste your time trying to write down everything that your professor says. Instead, listen closely and write down only the important points. Review these points after class to remind you of related points that were made during the lecture.

3. If the class discussion takes a spontaneous turn, pay attention and participate in the discussion. Only take notes on the conclusions that are relevant to the lecture.

4. Emphasize main points in your notes. You may want to use a highlighter, special notation (asterisks, exclamation points), format (circle, underline), or placement on the page (indented, bulleted). You will find that when you try to recall these points, you will be able to actually picture them on the page.

5. Be sure to copy specific formulas, laws, and theories word-for-word.

6. Hearing something repeated, stressed, or summed up can be a signal that it is an important concept to understand.

7. Organize handouts, study guides, and exams in your notebook along with your lecture notes. It may be helpful to use a three-ring binder, so that you can insert pages wherever you need to.

8. When taking notes, you might find it helpful to leave a wide margin on all four sides of the page. Doing this allows you to note names, dates, definitions, etc. for easy access and studying later. It may also be helpful to make notes of questions you want to ask your professor about or research later, ideas or relationships that you may want to explore more on your own, or concepts that you don't fully understand.

9. It is best to maintain a separate notebook for each class. Labeling and dating your notes can be helpful when you need to look up information from previous lectures.

10. Make your notes legible, and take notes directly in your notebook. Chances are you won't recopy them no matter how noble your intentions. Spend the time you would have spent recopying the notes studying them instead, drawing conclusions and making connections that you didn't have time for in class.

11. Look over your notes after class while the lecture is still fresh in your mind. Fix illegible items and clarify anything you don't understand. Do this again right before the next class.

Chapter 1: Introducing the Dimensions of Human Sexuality

Learning Objectives

By the end of this chapter, you should be able to:

- Identify and discuss the dimensions of human sexuality, including biological, psychological, and sociocultural factors.

- Discuss the historical aspects of human sexuality, including the sexual revolution, the role of gender, and the role of culture.

- Apply critical thinking methods to human sexuality.

- Outline the reasons to study human sexuality, including the steps of the decision-making process.

Notes

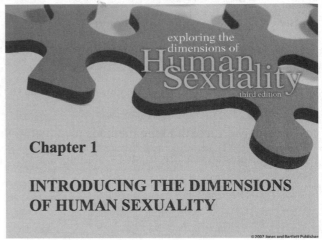

Chapter 1

INTRODUCING THE DIMENSIONS OF HUMAN SEXUALITY

© 2007 Jones and Bartlett Publishers

IN OTHERS' WORDS...

- "After people are clothed and fed, then they think about sex."

  —K'ung Fu-Tzu (Confucius)
  551–479 BC

© 2007 Jones and Bartlett Publishers

CHAPTER OBJECTIVES

- Identify and discuss the dimensions of human sexuality, including biological, psychological, and sociocultural factors.
- Discuss the historical aspects of human sexuality, including the sexual revolution, the role of gender, and the role of culture.

© 2007 Jones and Bartlett Publishers

Notes

_____

_____

_____

_____

_____

_____

_____

_____

_____

_____

_____

_____

_____

_____

_____

_____

_____

_____

_____

_____

_____

_____

_____

_____

_____

_____

_____

_____

_____

_____

_____

CHAPTER OBJECTIVES

- Apply critical thinking methods to human sexuality.
- Outline the reasons to study human sexuality, including the steps of the decision-making process.

©2007 Jones and Bartlett Publisher

THE DIMENSIONS OF HUMAN SEXUALITY

- The interactive nature of sexual dimensions
- Biological dimension *(Physiology of sex)*
- Psychological dimension
- Sociocultural factors

©2007 Jones and Bartlett Publisher

IN OTHERS' WORDS…

- "Sex is hardly ever just about sex."
  —*Shirley Maclaine*

©2007 Jones and Bartlett Publisher

THE DIMENSIONS OF HUMAN SEXUALITY

- Biological dimension *(Physiology of sex)*
  - *Gender*
  - *Genetics*
  - *Reproduction*
  - *Fertility control*
  - *Sexual arousal and response*
  - *Physiological cycles and changes*
  - *Physical appearance*
  - *Growth and development*

©2007 Jones and Bartlett Publishers

THE DIMENSIONS OF HUMAN SEXUALITY

- Psychological dimension
  - *Emotions*
  - *Experiences*
  - *Self-concept*
  - *Motivation*
  - *Expressiveness*
  - *Learned attitudes and behaviors*
  - *Body image*

©2007 Jones and Bartlett Publishers

THE DIMENSIONS OF HUMAN SEXUALITY

- Sociocultural dimension
  - *Religious influences*
  - *Multicultural influences*
  - *Socioeconomic influences (income, education)*
  - *Ethical influences*
  - *Media influences*
  - *Political policy*

©2007 Jones and Bartlett Publishers

IN OTHERS' WORDS...

- "Sex. In America an obsession. In other parts of the world a fact."
  —*Marlene Dietrich*

©2007 Jones and Bartlett Publisher

HISTORICAL INFLUENCES ON SEXUALITY

- Sexual revolution
- Control of sexual behavior
- Conception
- Contraception
- Gender roles
- Multicultural dimensions
  - *Polygamy*

©2007 Jones and Bartlett Publisher

THINKING CRITICALLY ABOUT HUMAN SEXUALITY

- Correlation versus causation
- Being a good consumer of sexual information

©2007 Jones and Bartlett Publisher

Notes

_____

_____

_____

_____

_____

_____

_____

_____

_____

_____

_____

_____

_____

_____

_____

_____

_____

_____

_____

_____

_____

_____

_____

_____

_____

_____

_____

_____

_____

_____

_____

_____

_____

_____

_____

_____

WHY STUDY SEXUALITY?

- Sexual knowledge
- Personal values
- Responsible sexual decision making

©2007 Jones and Bartlett Publishers

WHY STUDY SEXUALITY?

- Decision-making model
  - Recognition (precisely defining the issue at hand)
  - Evaluation (gather information and determine best scenario)
  - Implementation (put plan into action)
  - Review (evaluating the effectiveness of the plan)

©2007 Jones and Bartlett Publishers

WHY STUDY SEXUALITY?

- Sexual health and wellness *(reducing and/or eliminating risks)*
- Service–learning projects in your community

©2007 Jones and Bartlett Publishers

DIMENSIONS OF SEXUALITY

- Biological factors
  - *Gender*
  - *Genetics*
  - *Reproduction*
  - *Fertility control*
  - *Arousal and response*
  - *Physiological cycles and changes*
  - *Growth and development*

© 2007 Jones and Bartlett Publisher

DIMENSIONS OF SEXUALITY

- Psychological factors
  - *Emotions*
  - *Experience*
  - *Self-concept*
  - *Motivation*
  - *Expressiveness*
  - *Learned attitudes and behaviors*
  - *Body image*

© 2007 Jones and Bartlett Publisher

DIMENSIONS OF SEXUALITY

- Sociocultural factors
  - *Socioeconomic status*
  - *Laws*
  - *Religion*
  - *Culture*
  - *Ethnic heritage*
  - *Media and ad information*
  - *Family, neighborhoods, friends*
  - *Ethics*

© 2007 Jones and Bartlett Publisher

Chapter 1 Summary: Fill in the Blanks

The Dimensions of Human Sexuality

We define human sexuality as part of your total personality, a natural part of life. It involves the interrelationship of biological, psychological, and sociocultural dimensions. The Sexuality Information and Education Council of the United States (SIECUS) defines human sexuality as: _____

_____

_____.

The *biological dimension* includes basic physiology and genetics. The *psychological dimension* refers to our sense of well-being. The _____ *dimension* is the sum of cultural and social influences that affect our sexual thoughts and actions. Such influences may be religious, multicultural and global, ethical and legal, political, or derive from socioeconomic status or media input. The media help shape public attitudes on many topics, including sexuality, gender roles, and sexual behaviors.

Historical Influences

The sexual revolution appears to be an evolution that began before the 1900s. More recent events, such as more reliable contraceptives and a greater acceptance of sexuality in public forums, continue the evolution. Attempts to control sexual behavior through history have included declaring certain behaviors "unnatural," claiming that lust and passion came from evil spirits, legislating against a variety of behaviors, and using religion as a means to prohibit certain behaviors. Because our ancestors did not understand contraception, a number of explanations for childbirth arose. Until the end of the 1800s no one really knew how conception occurred. The ability to control reproduction today is taken for granted, but throughout most of history this was not the case. The advent of reliable contraceptive methods, particularly the Pill in the _____s, separated the act of sexual intercourse from reproduction.

Thinking Critically About Human Sexuality

Critical thinking—thinking that avoids blind acceptance of conclusions or arguments and closely examines all assumptions—is important to being able to understand and interpret information related to sexuality. A _____ shows that a relationship exists between two events. A _____ shows that one event caused the other. Being a good consumer of sexual information means evaluating studies before accepting their conclusions, as well as thinking about why someone is publishing the study.

Why Study Sexuality?

We study human sexuality to acquire a strong foundation of sexual knowledge and to understand sexual attitudes. Such information, self-knowledge, and understanding can help people make reasonable and responsible sexual decisions. Understanding sexuality promotes well-being by relieving anxieties and by promoting sexual health. Steps in the decision-making process are 1) _____, 2) _____, 3) _____, and 4) _____. Service-learning is an educational method by which students learn through active participation in an organized service experience.

Review the Dimensions

Match the following to the appropriate **dimension of sexuality** as described in your text.

a. Biological   b. Psychological   c. Sociocultural

1. Spinal cord injury _____
2. Ethnicity _____
3. Education _____
4. Music or TV _____
5. Your sense of being _____
6. Genetics _____
7. Socioeconomic status _____
8. Anatomy & physiology _____
9. Religion _____
10. Human sexual response cycle _____

Focus on the Facts

Use the following table to help organize your review of the sexuality related research studies found in this chapter.

Researchers/Topic	Findings or statistics, and notes to help you remember.
Dimensions of Sexuality *Biological* *Psychological* *Sociocultural* p. 4–14	
Historical-Cultural Influences *The sexual revolution* *Control of behavior* *Conception* *Contraception* *Gender roles* p. 14–24	
Correlation Versus Causation p. 24–25	

Researchers/Topic	Findings or statistics, and notes to help you remember.
Consumer of Sex Information p. 27–28	
Why Study Sexuality p. 27–31	
Service Learning p. 31	

Quick Questions

Describe one current sexuality issue and how it relates to each of the dimensions of human sexuality (biological, psychological and sociocultural).

What connection did Laumann and associates find between sexual behavior and religiosity? (hint, look at page 8)

After reading about the historical-cultural influences on sexuality, which area do you find most interesting and why?

Activity 1.3: Autobiography "The Sexual You" Journal

The purpose of this activity is to provide an opportunity to evaluate yourself as a sexual person. By exploring your feelings openly (in writing) you may experience a reduction of fears and embarrassments. You may also develop some new understanding or appreciation of your own behavior and/or that of someone close to you, and you may find solutions or alternatives to meet the requirements of your own situations. This activity should deal more with your *psychological being* rather than a chronology of what you did with whom.

You may include the following in this assignment:

- Your relationship with your family from childhood until now

- Your relationships with friends, lovers and other significant people in your life

- Your personal choices, what influences them, who influences them

- Dramatic or important realizations or events

- Your feelings about yourself, your gender, your body

- Your feelings on why you are attracted to the person/persons to whom you are attracted

- Your sexual orientation and your feeling about the orientation of others

- Your hopes for the future with finding a partner, having children, your sexual health, etc.

- Anything else you wish to include

- What you want to learn from this class and why you enrolled

Activity 1.4: WEB-EX

Access the *Making the Connection: Sexuality and Reproductive Health Definitions of Sexually Related Health Terminology* through the "Want to know more?" section on the text web site below or at *www.siecus.org/pubs/cnct/ cnct0001.html.* Explain the following concepts:

Sexually Healthy Adult-

Sexually Healthy Relationship-

Sexual Rights-

Want to know more? You can find additional information about topics covered in this chapter at sexuality.jbpub.com.

Chapter 2: Sexuality Research

Learning Objectives

By the end of this chapter, you should be able to:

- Describe the various methods used in sexuality research, including the steps in the scientific process.
- Identify the ethical issues involved in sexuality research.
- Describe the work of early sexuality researchers and how they set the stage for modern research.
- Summarize the contributions of major modern sexuality researchers.

Chapter 2

SEXUALITY RESEARCH

© 2007 Jones and Bartlett Publisher

CHAPTER OBJECTIVES

- Describe the various methods used in sexuality research, including the steps in the scientific process.
- Identify the ethical issues involved in sexuality research.
- Describe the work of early sexuality researchers and how they set the stage for modern research.
- Summarize the contributions of major modern sexuality researchers.

© 2007 Jones and Bartlett Publisher

RESEARCH METHODS:
Scientific Method

- Identifying a research question
- Reviewing the literature
- Formulating a hypothesis
- Operationalizing variables
- Collecting data
- Analyzing the data to test the hypothesis

© 2007 Jones and Bartlett Publisher

Notes

_____

_____

_____

_____

_____

_____

_____

_____

_____

_____

_____

_____

_____

_____

_____

_____

_____

_____

_____

_____

_____

_____

_____

_____

_____

_____

_____

_____

_____

_____

_____

_____

_____

_____

RESEARCH METHODS:
Survey Research

- Self-report data
  - May include inaccuracies
    - Difficulty recalling past events
    - Embellishment
    - Estimation
- Questionnaires
  - Less expensive than interviews
  - Convenience makes people feel more relaxed and reinforces anonymity
- Interviews
  - Individuals may be embarrassed

©2007 Jones and Bartlett Publishers

RESEARCH METHODS:
Case Studies

- In-depth studies of individuals
- Small select group
- Group is followed over a period of time

Photo © BananaStock/Alamy Images

©2007 Jones and Bartlett Publishers

RESEARCH METHODS:
Experimental Research

- Behavior studied under controlled conditions
- Common design includes two groups
  - Experimental group
  - Control group
- Control over variable thought to influence response or behavior

©2007 Jones and Bartlett Publishers

RESEARCH METHODS:
Direct Observation

- Subjects watched in a laboratory, a class, a natural setting, or in the workplace

© 2007 Jones and Bartlett Publishers

ISSUES IN SEXUALITY
RESEARCH

- Ethical issues
  - Informed consent
  - Confidentiality
  - Racial issues
- Validity
  - Testing what is supposed to be tested

Courtesy of Behavioral Technology

© 2007 Jones and Bartlett Publishers

EARLY SEXUAL
RESEARCHERS

- Richard von Krafft-Ebing (1840–1902)

- Henry Havelock Ellis (1859–1939)

- Sigmund Freud (1856–1939)

© 2007 Jones and Bartlett Publishers

Notes

_____
_____
_____
_____
_____
_____
_____
_____
_____
_____
_____
_____
_____
_____
_____
_____
_____
_____
_____
_____
_____
_____
_____
_____
_____
_____
_____
_____
_____
_____
_____
_____
_____
_____
_____

RICHARD VON KRAFFT-EBING (1840–1902)

- Physician who worked primarily with sexually disturbed people
- Supported what we know as the double standard
  - Whereby men have sexual freedoms, women do not.
- Writings had tremendous influence on many physicians

© 2007 Jones and Bartlett Publishers

HENRY HAVELOCK ELLIS (1859–1939)

- English psychologist and physician
- Published *Studies in the Psychology of Sex*
  - Masturbation is common for both sexes
  - Orgasm in males and females is same
  - Homo/heterosexuality is a matter of degree
  - Women have sexual desire
  - No "norm" for human sexuality
  - Sex-Ed should start early
  - There should be no laws against contraception or private sexual behavior

© 2007 Jones and Bartlett Publishers

SIGMUND FREUD (1856–1939)

- Psychological researcher
- Developed theories about:
  - *Human development*
  - *Personality*
  - *Psychopathology*
- Viewed sexuality and sexual pleasure as a central part of human life
- Suggested that early childhood experiences had strong consequences on adult functioning

© 2007 Jones and Bartlett Publishers

Notes

MAGNUS HIRSHFELD
(1868–1935)

- German physician
- Homosexual and transvestite
- Founded the Medical Society for Sexology and Eugenics

©2007 Jones and Bartlett Publishers

KATHERINE DAVIS
(1860–1935)

- Improved conditions in penal institutions
- Public health opinion research found that:
  - Contraception approved in principle by almost 90% of respondents and practiced by 73%

Photo © Kimber Rey Solana/ShutterStock ©2007 Jones and Bartlett Publishers

20TH-CENTURY SEXUALITY RESEARCHERS / SCIENTIFIC LITERATURE

- Alfred C. Kinsey: **Establishing Scientific Sex Research**
- William Masters and Virginia Johnson: **The Physiology of Sexual Response**
- Robert Sorenson: **Adolescent Sexuality in the 1970s**
- Melvin Zelnik and John Kantner: **Sexual Behavior of Young Women**
- Alan Bell and Martin Weinberg: **Homosexuality**
- Philip Blumstein and Pepper Schwartz: **Relationships Among Couples**

©2007 Jones and Bartlett Publishers

ALFRED C. KINSEY: ESTABLISHING SCIENTIFIC SEX RESEARCH

- Biologist and zoologist
- Amassed information concerning sexual activities and beliefs about sexuality from students
- Sample comprised a disproportionately large number of educated, urban, Protestant young people

© 2007 Jones and Bartlett Publishers

WILLIAM MASTERS AND VIRGINIA JOHNSON: THE PHYSIOLOGY OF SEXUAL RESPONSE

- Masters a gynecologist; Johnson a psychologist
- First to observe sexual behaviors in a laboratory setting
- Major finding: the human sexual response

© 2007 Jones and Bartlett Publishers

ROBERT SORENSON: ADOLESCENT SEXUALITY IN THE 1970s

- Data gathered from 400 adolescents, 13 to 19 years old
- Findings showed dramatic increase in premarital coitus among adolescents
- Reported that 70% of total U.S. population in their late teens were involved in premarital intercourse

© 2007 Jones and Bartlett Publishers

MELVIN ZELNIK AND JOHN KANTNER: SEXUAL BEHAVIOR OF YOUNG WOMEN

- Gathered information on sexual activity, contraceptive use, premarital pregnancy, and abortion, using probability sampling techniques
- Found consistent increases in coital activity and pregnancy rates during the 1970s, despite greater contraception in 1979
- Studied the sexual behavior of young black and white females

©2007 Jones and Bartlett Publishers

ALAN BELL AND MARTIN WEINBERG: HOMOSEXUALITY

- Studied homosexual activity of men and women in San Francisco area (1978)
- Concluded that the term homosexual should really be homosexualities
- Found that distinct types of relationships exist

©2007 Jones and Bartlett Publishers

PHILIP BLUMSTEIN AND PEPPER SCHWARTZ: RELATIONSHIPS AMONG COUPLES

- Published *American Couples*, 1983
- Found that both heterosexual and homosexual cohabiting couples seemed to have fewer difficulties in their relationships than married heterosexual couples

©2007 Jones and Bartlett Publishers

THE NATIONAL HEALTH AND SOCIAL LIFE SURVEY

- Assessed incidence and prevalence of a broad range of sexual practices and attitudes within U.S. population
- Federal funding lost in 1991 when legislation banning federal funding for sexuality research was passed
- Private funding allowed study to proceed, but with limited sample size

© 2007 Jones and Bartlett Publisher

POPULAR LITERATURE

- Nancy Friday: *What Do Women and Men Fantasize About?* (mid-1970s)
- Morton Hunt: *Urban Adult Sexual Behavior* (1974)
- Carol Travis and Susan Sadd: *The Redbook Report on Female Sexuality* (1977)

© 2007 Jones and Bartlett Publisher

POPULAR LITERATURE (Continued)

- Shere Hite: *Women's Sexuality; Men's Sexuality* (1972–1976)
- Lorna Sarrel and Philip Sarrel: *The Redbook Report on Sexual Relationships*
- June Reinisch and Ruth Beasley: *The Kinsey Institute New Report on Sex*
- *NBC News* and *People* Magazine: *National Survey of Young Teens Sexual Attitudes and Behavior*

© 2007 Jones and Bartlett Publisher

Notes

_____

_____

_____

_____

_____

_____

_____

_____

_____

_____

_____

_____

_____

_____

_____

_____

_____

_____

_____

_____

_____

_____

_____

_____

_____

_____

_____

_____

_____

_____

_____

_____

_____

_____

_____

_____

OTHER EXAMPLES OF CURRENT RESEARCH

- Studies on ethnic differences in sexual attitudes and behavior
- Studies on the use of contraception
- Other representative studies
- Research on sexuality education

© 2007 Jones and Bartlett Publisher

BIOLOGICAL FACTORS AND SEX RESEARCH

- Medical model was focus of sexuality research in the 19th century.
- Sexual response cycle was discovered by the researchers Masters and Johnson.
- Physiological changes in the vagina or penis can be monitored by the vaginal plethysmograph and penile strain gauge.

© 2007 Jones and Bartlett Publisher

PSYCHOLOGICAL FACTORS AND SEX RESEARCH

- NHSLS data found married people were more likely to report being extremely or very happy.
- Behaviors and practices, as well as frequency, need to be accounted for in sexuality research.
- Motivation to respond to sex research may create bias.
- Learned attitudes and behaviors may influence answers on sex surveys.

© 2007 Jones and Bartlett Publisher

Notes

_____

_____

_____

_____

_____

_____

_____

_____

_____

_____

_____

_____

_____

_____

_____

_____

_____

_____

_____

_____

_____

_____

_____

_____

_____

_____

_____

_____

_____

_____

_____

_____

_____

_____

_____

SOCIOCULTURAL FACTORS AND SEX RESEARCH

- Gender "double standard" research goes back to 19th century.
- Education leads to both later age at 1st intercourse and higher use of contraception at 1st intercourse.
- Religious teens less likely to participate in sexual intercourse.
- Ethical considerations abound in sexuality research

©2007 Jones and Bartlett Publishers

Chapter 2 Summary: Fill in the Blanks

Research Methods

Sexuality research is usually conducted by _____ (using interviews and/or questionnaires), self-reports, observation, or experiment. The scientific method of research involves identifying a research question, reviewing the literature, formulating a hypothesis, operationalizing variables, collecting data, and analyzing the data to test the hypothesis.

Issues in Sexuality Research

Special problems are inherent in sexuality research owing to (a) the complexity of influences on sexuality; (b) subjects' inhibitions regarding sexual matters; (c) the difficulty of getting representative subjects; (d) subjects' difficulty in recalling early attitudes and experiences; and (e) personal biases on the parts of researchers and/or subjects. Participants in sexuality research must give their informed _____ before being used as research subjects.

Early sexuality research done by Krafft-Ebing, Ellis, and Freud was controversial, but their thinking about sexual attitudes and behavior provided the foundation for later research.

Twentieth-century sexuality researchers began to explore the psychological, psychosocial and physiological perspectives of sexuality. Although it was not the first sexuality study, Alfred Kinsey's large survey of human sexual behaviors in the United States established a systematic scientific approach to studying sexuality. Through laboratory observations, William _____ and Virginia _____ gathered information on human physiological responses to sexual stimulation. Their widely publicized and highly influential results showed a response cycle of four phases: excitement, plateau, orgasm, and resolution. A study of sexual dysfunction brought the relationship of the physiology and psychology of sexual response into focus. Masters and Johnson's study of homosexuality added to the sexuality literature in that it showed that homosexuals are like heterosexuals—individuals who have a variety of sexual concerns.

Robert Sorenson studied behaviors and attitudes of _____ and found them to be in search of relationships based on love, expressive of feelings of caring and affection, and cognizant of irresponsible sexual activity. Zelnik and Kantner studied sexual activity of teenage women in the 1970s, showing a consistent increase in sexual activity and a greater use of contraception but an increase in teenage pregnancy.

Bell and Weinberg studied _____ and found them to be much like heterosexuals in their desire for good relationships; well-adjusted homosexuals were as normal psychologically as well-adjusted heterosexuals.

The National _____ survey assessed the incidence and prevalence of a broad range of sexual practices and attitudes within the U.S. population. Popular literature is filled with studies about sexuality. Nancy Friday asked men and women about sexual fantasies, Morton Hunt gathered data on adult sexual practices, and "The Redbook Report on Female Sexuality" focused on sexual practices of women premaritally, maritally, and extramaritally. Shere Hite did two anecdotal studies showing that both men and women have a variety of preferences and desires related to their sexuality. Her 1987 book indicated that women felt oppressed and even abused by men. Sarrel and Sarrel in their 1980 Redbook survey queried readers about the quality of their relationships and found that those surveyed were, for the most part, happy in their sex lives. _____ played an important role in their relationships.

Countless sexuality research studies have been done in recent years. Common topics include premarital sexual attitudes and behavior, factors influencing the use of contraceptives, living styles, attitudes toward abortion, attitudes and behavior related to AIDS, and the effects of sexuality education programs. The National Survey of Family Growth (NSFG) is a multipurpose survey based on personal interviews with over 60,000 U.S. women 15–44 years of age. NSFG surveys designed to collect data on factors affecting pregnancy and women's health have been conducted periodically since 1973.

Review the Types of Studies Used in Sexology

Match the following to the appropriate **research study** or **sexology tool** as described in your text.

a. Survey

1. _____ Observation of behavior (or effects) under controlled conditions.

b. Scientific method

2. _____ Document required to participate in a research study after the purposes, risks, and benefits of the study have been explained.

c. Interview

3. _____ Research in which people are asked about their sexual attitudes and experiences. Can be oral or written.

d. Questionnaire

4. _____ In-depth study of individual(s) or small groups, to look at specific behaviors or characteristics in great depth.

e. Informed consent

5. _____ Research conducted in an atmosphere free from bias.

f. Self-report data

6. _____ Oral research method designed to gather information.

g. Case study

7. _____ A laboratory measuring device that charts physiological changes over time.

h. Objectivity

8. _____ Respondents descriptions of something.

i. Experiment

9. _____ A written instrument designed to gather data.

j. Plethysmograph

10. _____ Being sure the results are the same no matter who asks the questions or records the answers.

Focus on the Facts

Use the following table to help organize your review of the sexology researchers highlighted in this chapter.

Researchers	Contributions to sexuality research.
von Krafft-Ebing p. 47–48	
Ellis p. 48	
Freud p. 48	
Katherine Davis p. 49–50	
Kinsey p. 51–54	
Masters and Johnson p. 54–56	

Researchers	Contributions to sexuality research.
Sorenson p. 57	
Zelnik and Kanter p. 57–58	
Bell and Weinberg p. 58	
Blumstein and Schwartz p. 58–59	
NHSLS p. 59	
Friday p. 60	
Hunt p. 60	
Tarvis and Sadd p. 60–61	
Hite p. 60–63	
Sarrel and Sarrel p. 63	
Reinisch and Beasley p. 63–64	
Seventeen Magazine and Kaiser Family Foundation p. 64	
NBC News and *People Magazine* p. 64–66	
Other Studies Karofsky, 2001 p. 69	

Test Your Knowledge. Are the Following Statements True or False?

Page numbers are provided to help you check your answers as you study.

1. True   False   Sexuality should be researched in an atmosphere free from bias to give an objective view of the issues examined. (p. 40)

2. True   False   Individuals who volunteer to participate in sexuality research are good representatives of the general public. (p. 41)

3. True   False   Experimental Research allows control over variables thought to influence responses or behavior. (p. 43)

4. True   False   Plethysmography uses a tool to measure changes in heart rate during sexual excitement. (p. 46)

5. True   False   H. Havelock Ellis approached sexuality research from a psychoanalytical perspective. (p. 48)

6. True   False   Alfred Kinsey wrote *Sexual Behavior in the Human Male* in 1948. (p. 52)

7. True   False   The work of Masters and Johnson helped describe the physiological changes in the human sexual response cycle. (p. 54–56)

8. True   False   The National Health and Social Life Survey (NHSLS) was the first comprehensive survey of adult sexual behavior. (p. 59)

Activity 2.1: Sexuality Research in Popular Culture

We learn about sexuality from a number of different sources. Magazines and newspapers often report findings of sexuality research. Some even use it to titillate and entice you to buy the magazine. Find a sexuality based research study from a magazine or newspaper. Clip or copy it and attach it to a short critique of the research. Highlight the flaws and strengths of the article based on the criteria discussed in your text. (Check out "Communication Dimensions" on page 60 for some ideas!) Finally, should you believe what you read in this research? Why or why not?

Activity 2.2: Studying Sexuality

Using the steps in the scientific method, highlight a research study you would like to see conducted in the field of sexology. Be sure to include a brief description of the six steps you would take to conduct this study.

Want to know more? You can find additional information about topics covered in this chapter at sexuality.jbpub.com.

Learning Objectives

By the end of this chapter, you should be able to:

- Describe the process of sexual communication, including nonverbal communication.

- Identify barriers to sexual communication, including gender, attitudes about sexuality, and sexual language.

- Discuss techniques for improving sexual communication.

Chapter 3

SEXUAL COMMUNICATION

© 2007 Jones and Bartlett Publisher

CHAPTER OBJECTIVES

- Describe the process of sexual communication, including nonverbal communication.
- Identify barriers to sexual communication, including gender, attitudes about sexuality, and sexual language.
- Discuss techniques for improving sexual communication.

© 2007 Jones and Bartlett Publisher

IN OTHERS' WORDS...

- "Listen or thy tongue will keep thee deaf."

  —*Indian proverb*

© 2007 Jones and Bartlett Publisher

THE PROCESS OF COMMUNICATING SEXUALLY

- Basic communication model
  - *Five steps*
- Nonverbal communication
  - *Unwritten and unspoken*
- Gender communication issues
  - *Differences in men and women*

© 2007 Jones and Bartlett Publishers

IN OTHERS' WORDS…

- "When the eyes say one thing, and the tongue another, a practiced man relies on the language of the first."

  —*Ralph Waldo Emerson*

© 2007 Jones and Bartlett Publishers

BASIC COMMUNICATION MODEL

Basic Communication Model

| 1. Sender has idea | → | 2. Sender encodes message | → | 3. Channel carries message | → | 4. Receiver decodes message |

5. Feedback

© 2007 Jones and Bartlett Publishers

Notes

_____
_____
_____
_____
_____
_____
_____
_____
_____
_____
_____
_____
_____
_____
_____
_____
_____
_____
_____
_____
_____
_____
_____
_____
_____
_____
_____
_____
_____
_____
_____
_____
_____
_____
_____

BARRIERS TO EFFECTIVE SEXUAL COMMUNICATION

- Bypassing
- Frame of reference
- Lack of language skills
- Lack of listening skills
- Mind-altering drugs
- Attitudes about sexuality
- Sexual language

© 2007 Jones and Bartlett Publisher

GENDER COMMUNICATION ISSUES

He says  She says

- Vocabulary differences
- Gender roles
- Expressing feelings
- Learned or real differences?

Photo © Creatas
© 2007 Jones and Bartlett Publisher

OTHER COMMUNICATION ISSUES

- Attitudes about sexuality
- Parent–teen communication
  - 90% of parents say they do not know how to discuss sexuality with their children
- Sexual language

© Photos.com
© 2007 Jones and Bartlett Publisher

Notes

TECHNIQUES FOR IMPROVING SEXUAL COMMUNICATION

- Planning
- Flooding
- Learning assertiveness
  - DESC model of assertiveness

© 2007 Jones and Bartlett Publishers

TECHNIQUES FOR IMPROVING SEXUAL COMMUNICATION

- Assertiveness: Standing up for your rights without violating the rights of others.
- Aggressiveness: Standing up for your rights at the expense of someone else's rights.
- Nonassertiveness: Giving up your basic rights so that other people can achieve theirs.

© 2007 Jones and Bartlett Publishers

TECHNIQUES FOR IMPROVING SEXUAL COMMUNICATION

- Expressing yourself nonverbally
- Seeking information
- Steps towards change
  - "I" Statements
  - Active listening

© 2007 Jones and Bartlett Publishers

TECHNIQUES FOR IMPROVING SEXUAL COMMUNICATION

- Resolving conflicts
  - Identify the interests
  - Identify higher levels of interest
  - Create an agreement frame
  - Brainstorm for solutions
- Giving and receiving criticism
  - Can improve relationships by fostering communication
  - Express emotions such as love, caring, and wonderment

© 2007 Jones and Bartlett Publishers

IN OTHERS' WORDS...

- "Good communication is as stimulating as black coffee, and just as hard to sleep after."

  —*Anne Morrow Lindbergh*

Photo © Art-Line Productions/Brand X Pic   © 2007 Jones and Bartlett Publishers

BIOLOGICAL FACTORS AND COMMUNICATION

- Physiological reactions, like blushing or erections, are nonverbal means of communicating sexual attraction.
- Alcohol or drugs can distort the communication process.
- Physical touching can indicate interest, intimacy, and emotional closeness.
- Hearing loss over time can inhibit communication and frustrate a partner.

© 2007 Jones and Bartlett Publishers

PSYCHOLOGICAL FACTORS AND COMMUNICATION

- Emotions can overwhelm the ability to communicate.
- Double standard may alter communication process.
- Ego may get in the way of listening to a partner.
- Self-image and body image may distort communication.

© 2007 Jones and Bartlett Publisher

SOCIOCULTURAL FACTORS AND COMMUNICATION

- Media strongly influence sexual communication.
- Gender affects style of communication.
- Sexuality education may increase confidence.
- Cultures influence communication style.
- Family and peers set example of sexuality communication.

© 2007 Jones and Bartlett Publisher

Chapter 3 Summary: Fill in the Blanks

The Process of Communicating Sexually

The basic communication process consists of a sender having an idea, the sender _____ the idea into a message, the message traveling over a _____, the receiver decoding the message, and the receiver responding with _____. Nonverbal communication, consisting of all unwritten and unspoken messages, includes body language, touch, facial expressions, use of hands, and vocal inflection. Up to _____% of message meaning may be sent nonverbally.

Barriers to Effective Sexual Communication

Most messages reach their destination, but are misunderstood due to communication barriers. The most common barriers are _____, frame of reference, lack of language skills, lack of listening skills, and _____. Another barrier to effective sexual communication is gender differences in communication style. Tannen indicates that women consult with their partners throughout the decision-making process, while men make more decisions _____. Many people are uncomfortable with sexual language. Some sexual words evoke such strong emotions that they create a barrier to effective communication.

Techniques for Improving Sexual Communication

Sexual communication can be improved if partners are willing to try some of the following techniques. Planning involves setting aside time to talk about sexual issues, approaching the discussion with the goal of _____, and allowing time for changes to happen. Flooding involves standing in front of a mirror, looking yourself in the eye, and repeating sexual words that make you feel uncomfortable until you are able to use them. Learning assertiveness involves learning to _____ _____.

The DESC method involves: 1) _____, 2) expressing your feelings about the behavior, 3) specifying changes you would like to see made, and 4) _____ _____.

Expressing yourself _____ includes adding smiles, winks, hugs, touches, kisses, or other ways to communicate your affection. Listen actively to your partner, and ask whether your understanding of your partner's feelings and intentions is accurate. Steps toward improving sexual relations include active listening, eliciting feedback from your partner, expressing feelings and thoughts directly, and using "_____" statements. Conflict resolution can be facilitated with effective communication. Learn to give and receive criticism in a nonthreatening manner.

Focus on the Facts

Use the following table to help organize your review of the sexual communication issues highlighted in this chapter.

Issues	Type of research, findings, or statistics, and notes to help you remember

Process of Communicating Sexually
  Model
  Nonverbal
p. 94–98	

Barriers to Effective Communication
  Gender issues
  Attitudes
  Parent-teen
  Sexual language
p. 98–105	

Improving Sexual Communication
  Planning
  Flooding
  Assertiveness
  Nonverbal
  Listening
  "I" statements
  Resolving conflict
  Criticism
p. 106–115	

Match the Following to the Appropriate Communication Tool as Described in Your Text.

a. Feedback

b. Decoding

c. Bypassing

d. Encoding

e. Flooding

f. Aggressiveness

g. Nonassertiveness

h. Assertiveness

i. Active listening

j. "I" statements

1. _____ Statements that express personal feelings.

2. _____ Standing up for one's basic rights, but at the expense of someone else's basic rights.

3. _____ Giving up your basic rights so others may achieve theirs.

4. _____ When the receiver responds verbally or nonverbally.

5. _____ Standing up for one's basic rights without violating anyone else's rights.

6. _____ Translating the message from its symbol form into meaning.

7. _____ Converting an idea into words or gestures to convey meaning.

8. _____ Experiencing something so frequently that you no longer are aroused by it. Used to become more comfortable with sexual terminology.

9. _____ When misunderstandings result from missed meanings.

10. _____ Paraphrasing what someone has said to demonstrate interest and understanding.

Activity 3.1: Did You Ever Feel Like You Were Talking to Yourself?

Fill in the following table with different types of listeners. Next, jot a few notes to describe a situation that you may have used or had others use these characteristics on you. How did you feel in that situation?

Type of listener	Description	Situation
Ex. *Placater*	Agreeing with everything you hear just to be nice or to prevent conflict.	
	Drifting off during a conversation.	
	You hear little or nothing but wonder "what is he/she really thinking?"	
	You hear what's said, but quickly belittle or discount it.	
	Hearing only what you want to hear.	
	Changing the subject too quickly tells others you are not interested.	
	Referring everything you hear to your experience.	
	You mentally try out what you will say next and tune out the speaker.	
	When you get side-tracked assessing the messenger.	

Describe a situation where you felt someone important was not listening to what you were trying to say. How did that make you feel?

What steps can you identify to improve your listening skills with people you care about?

Activity 3.2: Conflict Resolution

Explain the following conflict resolution concepts (p. 112):

1. Active listening:

2. Identifying your position:

3. Proposing and exploring alternative solutions:

4. What should you consider when giving criticism?

5. What should you remember when receiving criticism?

Activity 3.3: Talking About Sex, Then and Now

While this course and text will teach you the proper terminology for sexual anatomy, physiology and behaviors, we often grow up with our own expressions and words that we are most comfortable with for these topics.

When you were a child, what words did you feel comfortable with for the following?

Female Anatomy	Male Anatomy	Sexual Functions	Sexual Behaviors

How do you feel using these words now? Have you changed your sexual vocabulary as you matured? What factors may have influenced your change in terms?

Explain whether you feel more comfortable with slang terms or proper vocabulary with the following individuals or groups. Why?

Your parents-

A significant love interest-

Your friends-

If you think you may have children some day, what terms do you think you will use with them?

Activity 3.4: WEB-EX

Personality and Communication

The purpose of this assignment is to help you better understand your temperament and that of someone you care about. You are to select another person to participate in this activity with you. This other person should be someone you have a relationship with; a loved one, a roommate, a best friend, a parent. Good communication in your relationship with this other person is important. When you have an understanding of how your temperament fits into your relationship, you can begin to find ways to improve your communication with this other person to:

- **build stronger relationships** by improving your communication and interpersonal skills

- **meet others' expectations** by better understanding people's styles and preferences

- **diffuse interpersonal problems** by gaining new sensitivity to others' perspectives

- **achieve valuable self-knowledge** into your core motivations and behaviors

You and a significant other with whom you must communicate, should go to the following web address: *www.keirsey.com.*

Take the Keirsey Temperament Sorter test. (The online free version is enough to complete this assignment, but you could choose to pay for more in-depth results.) Go to the main page at the web address and look at the information about

- Love and Temperament (*http://keirsey.com/pygmalion/mirroroffiction.html*) and

- Mating and Temperament (*http://keirsey.com/pygmalion/couples.html*).

Complete the following questions after reviewing the characteristics of your temperament and that of your partner in this assignment.

Your temperament: Your partner's temperament:

_____   _____

General characteristics of the temperament types identified:

You-   Your partner-

Do you agree with this description of your personalities and temperaments? If no, why not?

After reading Love and Temperament and Mating and Temperament, what differences or similarities in your temperaments should you be aware of?

How might your temperaments influence your communication with the person who completed this assignment with you?

Activity 3.5: 3-D Sexual Communication

Your ability to communicate sexually is influenced by many factors. After reading this chapter, describe how the following factors may have helped or hindered your ability to communicate in a relationship. (This relationship could be a significant love interest or roommate, parent, or perhaps even a best friend.)

Biological Factors and Communication:

Psychological Factors and Communication:

Sociocultural Factors and Communication:

Want to know more? You can find additional information about topics covered in this chapter at sexuality.jbpub.com.

Learning Objectives

By the end of this chapter, you should be able to:

- Name and describe the parts of the female reproductive system, including external and internal genitalia.

- Discuss the role of breasts in sexual arousal and response, as well as in the reproductive function of lactation.

- Explain the role of hormones as they pertain to sexuality.

- Describe what occurs during menstruation, to include menarche, the menstrual cycle, perimenopause, and problems associated with each.

- Cite various diseases that can affect the female reproductive system and the self-care procedures, as well as medical treatments, associated with these diseases.

Chapter 4

**FEMALE SEXUAL ANATOMY
AND PHYSIOLOGY**

© 2007 Jones and Bartlett Publishers

CHAPTER OBJECTIVES

- Name and describe the parts of the female reproductive system, including external and internal genitalia.
- Discuss the role of breasts in sexual arousal and response, as well as in the reproductive function of lactation.
- Explain the role of hormones as they pertain to sexuality.

© 2007 Jones and Bartlett Publishers

CHAPTER OBJECTIVES

- Describe what occurs during menstruation, including menarche, the menstrual cycle, perimenopause, and problems associated with each.
- Cite various diseases that can affect the female reproductive system and the self-care procedures and medical treatments associated with these diseases.

© 2007 Jones and Bartlett Publishers

Notes

_____
_____
_____
_____
_____
_____
_____
_____
_____
_____
_____
_____
_____
_____
_____
_____
_____
_____
_____
_____
_____
_____
_____
_____
_____
_____
_____
_____
_____
_____
_____
_____

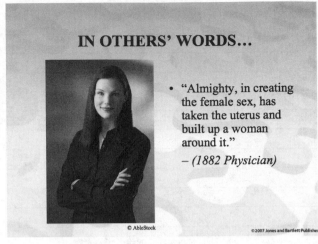

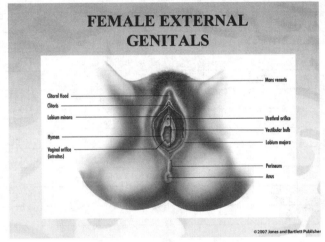

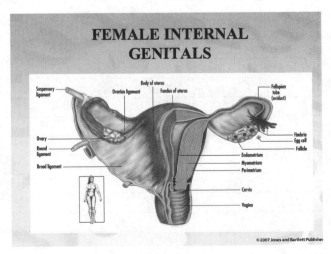

Notes

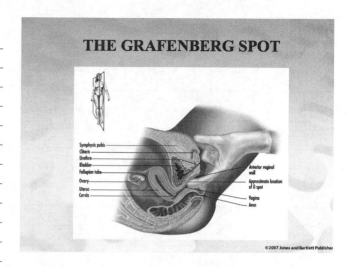

THE GRAFENBERG SPOT

Symphysis pubis
Clitoris
Urethra
Bladder
Fallopian tube
Ovary
Uterus
Cervix

Anterior vaginal wall
Approximate location of G spot
Vagina
Anus

© 2007 Jones and Bartlett Publishers

THE BREASTS

- Mammary glands
  - Clusters of milk-secreting structures
- Prolactin
  - Hormone that stimulates the production of breast milk
- Areola
  - Darkened skin around nipple

© 2007 Jones and Bartlett Publishers

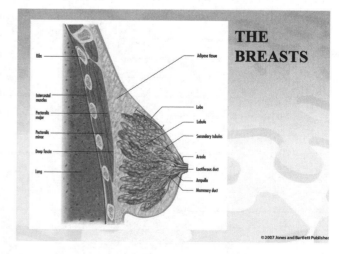

THE BREASTS

Ribs
Intercostal muscles
Pectoralis major
Pectoralis minor
Deep fascia
Lung

Adipose tissue
Lobe
Lobule
Secondary tubules
Areola
Lactiferous duct
Ampulla
Mammary duct

© 2007 Jones and Bartlett Publishers

Notes

THE HORMONES

- Endocrine glands
  - Glands that secrete their products into the bloodstream
- Hormones
  - Chemical substance secreted by a ductless gland

© 2007 Jones and Bartlett Publisher

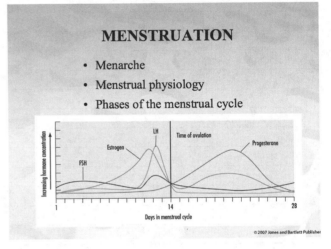

MENSTRUATION

- Menarche
- Menstrual physiology
- Phases of the menstrual cycle

© 2007 Jones and Bartlett Publisher

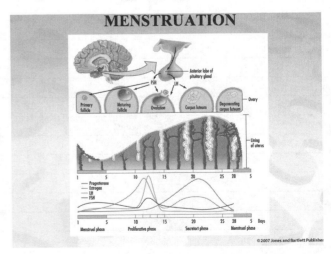

MENSTRUATION

© 2007 Jones and Bartlett Publisher

PHASES OF THE MENSTRUAL CYCLE

- Proliferative phase
- Secretory/Luteal phase
- Ovulatory phase
- Menstrual phase

© 2007 Jones and Bartlett Publisher

MENSTRUAL PROBLEMS

- Dysmenorrhea (primary and secondary)
- Amenorrhea (primary and secondary)
- Premenstrual syndrome (PMS)
- Endometriosis
- Menstrual cycle and sex

© 2007 Jones and Bartlett Publisher

PREGNANCY AND LACTATION

- Hormonal influences
  - High levels of prolactin

© Photodisc

© 2007 Jones and Bartlett Publisher

MENOPAUSE

- Symptoms of perimenopause and menopause
  - Headaches
  - Dizziness
  - Palpitations
  - Insomnia
  - Anxiety
- Treatment for menopause
- Hormone therapy

© 2007 Jones and Bartlett Publisher

SEXUALLY RELATED DISEASES: FEMALE REPRODUCTIVE SYSTEM

- Breasts
- Cervix
- Uterus
- Ovaries

© 2007 Jones and Bartlett Publisher

SEXUALLY RELATED DISEASES: SELF-CARE AND PREVENTION

- Genital self-examination (GSE)
- Breast self-examination (BSE)
- Care from medical specialists (gynecology)
- Care from organizations and available publications

© 2007 Jones and Bartlett Publisher

FEMALES AND BIOLOGICAL FACTORS

- Chromosomes and genetics
- Female physical appearance changes at puberty.
- Hormonal changes affect mood.
- Menopause
  - Lower estrogen levels increase risk of heart disease.

© 2007 Jones and Bartlett Publisher

FEMALES AND PSYCHOLOGICAL FACTORS

- Women have twice the rate of depression compared with men.
- Teen women w/low self-concept are more likely to have unwanted pregnancy and birth.
- Expressiveness of emotions helps women stay emotionally and physically healthy.

© 2007 Jones and Bartlett Publisher

FEMALES AND SOCIOCULTURAL FACTORS

- Socioeconomic status influences prenatal care and nutrition.
- Ethnic heritage influences women's health.
- Laws affect what health insurance is required to cover.
- Media and ads may influence eating patterns and health of women.

© 2007 Jones and Bartlett Publisher

Chapter 4 Summary: Fill in the Blanks

The Female Reproductive System

It is as important to know about sexual anatomy and reproductive functioning as it is to know about any other part of your body. Many individuals know more about how their cars work than how their bodies function. The external female genitals (the vulva) consist of the mons pubis, labia majora, labia minora, clitoris, vestibule, and urethral opening. The clitoris, protected by the _____, is a very sensitive structure because of its abundance of nerve endings.

The internal female genitals consist of the vagina, uterus, fallopian tubes, and the ovaries. Large numbers of ova, or eggs, are present in each ovary at birth. They are released from the Graafian follicle cyclically and move through a _____ (where fertilization may occur) to the uterus, where they are either implanted or expelled. If fertilization occurs, the baby will exit through the vagina (birth canal).

The outer one-third of the vagina is where the nerve endings are located. Consequently, penis length is generally irrelevant to sexual satisfaction. Furthermore, the vagina contracts around any object inserted within it, making the width of the penis also generally irrelevant to the women's sexual satisfaction from coitus. Some experts believe there is a particular location—the _____—on the anterior wall of the vagina that is extrasensitive to manual stimulation. When stimulated at this location, some women exhibit a discharge thought to be equivalent to an ejaculate. However, there is disagreement regarding both the existence of any uniquely sensitive vaginal area or of a female prostate that would secrete an ejaculate.

The uterus consists of three layers: the _____, which is very elastic and enables the uterus to stretch during pregnancy; the _____, which is made up of smooth muscle that helps push the newborn through the cervix; and the _____, which is loaded with blood vessels and provides the nourishment necessary to sustain a developing baby.

The Breasts

Breasts have significance in sexual arousal as well as in providing milk for the newborn baby. The stimulation of the newborn sucking on the nipple causes the pituitary gland to secrete prolactin, stimulating production of breast milk.

Hormones

Hormones are _____ secreted into the bloodstream by endocrine glands and carried to tissues and organs, which they stimulate (including other endocrine glands). Follicle-stimulating hormone (FSH) stimulates the ovary to ripen one ovum; _____ (LH) signals the Graafian follicle to release the ripened ovum; estrogens signal the _____ to release LH; progesterone released by the corpus luteum prepares the uterus for implantation of a fertilized ovum; androgens increase the sex drive; and _____ leads to the production of breast milk.

Menstruation

It is not entirely clear why menstruation begins (menarche). One hypothesis is that the increase in body fat that results from hormonal secretions during puberty "turns on" menstruation. Women begin menstruating at about _____ years of age. The menstrual cycle can be divided in several different ways. One method of division uses three phases: the proliferative phase, the secretory phase, and the menstrual phase. This method refers to occurrences in the uterus. Another method of classification uses changes in the ovaries as its basis. The categories in this method are the follicular phase, ovulation, and the luteal phase. Although menstrual cycles differ in length, the luteal phase—the phase from ovulation until menstruation—always is about _____ days long.

Menstrual problems may include dysmenorrhea, amenorrhea, or premenstrual syndrome (PMS). Dysmenorrhea is painful menstruation. Dysmenorrhea can be _____ —that is, _____or _____ in nature—that is, _____. PMS occurs just before and/or during menstruation and is associated with such symptoms as bloating, cramping, fatigue, depression, anxiety, headache, mood swings, crying spells, breast swelling, constipation, and joint pain.

There are many unanswered questions pertaining to PMS. One question relates to the cause of PMS, and another question pertains to the best way to treat it. Some suggest that PMS be treated with _____ and others advise counseling, sedatives, antidepressants, exercise, eliminating sugar and caffeine from the diet, herbal teas, reducing salt intake, or meditation or other relaxation techniques.

Contradictory data exist regarding the time of the menstrual cycle when women are most sexually aroused. Some researchers have found that women are most aroused just before menstruation, others say during menstruation, and still others have reported midcycle to be the time of greatest arousal.

There are no medical reasons why couples cannot engage in sexual intercourse during menstruation. Some refrain because of the messiness that may be involved and others because of religious taboos. If a couple chooses to engage in coitus, the woman can use a diaphragm to hold back the menstrual flow and the man can use a condom to prevent any irritation of the glans penis.

Hormones are also involved in pregnancy and lactation. During pregnancy the _____ _____ (HCG) is secreted from the placenta; the hormone prolactin stimulates the development of breast milk; and the hormone oxytocin is produced by the pituitary gland, allowing the breast milk to be ejected.

Menopause—_____—usually occurs between the ages of 40 and 55 and follows a five- to ten-year period of time called the perimenopause, or the climacteric. Menopause is due to the effects of aging on the ovaries, which no longer respond to the pituitary's command to produce sufficient amounts of estrogen and progesterone.

Hot flashes and vaginal dryness are two of the more disturbing potential symptoms of perimenopause and menopause. Hot flashes are sudden waves of heat felt from the waist up. Vaginal dryness is caused by the lowered amount of estrogen, which results in the vaginal walls shrinking and thinning and the vaginal mucosa becoming thinner. The result is that both the length and the width of the vagina become smaller, and vaginal lubrication decreases.

One controversial treatment for menopause is _____ (PHT). PHT may be related to endometrial cancer and breast cancer; however, at present it is administered with progestin, which results in the shedding of the endometrial lining, thereby decreasing the endometrial cancer threat. The effects of the long-term use of PHT are unknown.

Other treatments for menopause include antidepressants, changes in diet, exercise, keeping sexually active by engaging in coitus or masturbation, and using _____ such as K-Y or Lubifax water-soluble jellies.

Sexually Related Diseases: Self-Care and Prevention

Breast cancer is the second leading cancer in women and the second major cause of cancer death. Breast self-care includes monthly self-exams, clinical breast exams, and mammograms. Other breast disorders include cystic mastitis, fibroadenoma, nipple discharge, and breast abscess (infection). Incidence of cervical cancer has increased steadily.

Prevention includes annual _____. Annual gynecological examinations are recommended to diagnose any problems before they become major.

Match the Following Female Anatomical Parts, Functions and Health Concerns with the Appropriate Definitions

a. Pubococcygeal muscle

b. Primary dysmenorrhea

c. Postmenopause hormone therapy

d. Secondary dysmenorrhea

e. Graafian follicle

f. Corpus luteum

g. Late luteal phase dysphoric disorder

h. Endocrine glands

i. Primary amenorrhea

j. Interstitial-cell-stimulating hormone

k. Kegel exercises

1. _____ A part of the ovary from which a mature egg ruptures.

2. _____ A muscle that encircles and supports the vagina.

3. _____ A yellowish structure that develops in the Graafian follicle that produces progesterone.

4. _____ Treating menopausal women who have insufficient estrogen production with synthetic supplements.

5. _____ Glands that secrete their products into the bloodstream.

6. _____ Exercises to help women develop greater control of muscles supporting the genitalia.

7. _____ Painful menstruation caused by conditions such as endometriosis.

8. _____ Painful menstruation the cause of which is unknown.

9. _____ A hormone secreted by the pituitary that stimulated the production of sperm.

10. _____ A type of PMS in which mental and emotional symptoms occur the week before menstruation.

11. _____ A condition in which a woman age 18 or older has never menstruated.

Focus on the Facts

Use the following table to help organize your review of the female anatomy and physiology researchers highlighted in this chapter.

Topics	Type of research, findings, or statistics, and notes to help you remember.
External Genitals p. 124–127	
Internal Genitals p. 127–132	
Breasts p. 132–134	

Topics	Type of research, findings, or statistics, and notes to help you remember.
Hormones p. 134–135	
Menstruation p. 135–145	
Pregnancy and Lactation p. 146–147	
Menopause p. 147–151	
Self-Care and Prevention *Breasts* *Cervix* *Ovaries* *Vagina* *TSS* p. 151–162	

Learning anatomy and physiology, understanding the parts and how they function is complicated.

Want to know more? Are you confused yet? There are so many parts, inside and out, that many folks can't remember all the appropriate names. Some have never even seen many of the parts. Frankly, unless you are very flexible, it would be hard to see your own external genitalia without the use of a mirror. And what about the inside? The Human Sexuality Anatomy Review on the text web site will help you study human anatomy through interactive figure labeling exercises.

There are labeling exercises to help you learn all the female anatomy available at **sexuality.jbpub.com.**

Female systems provided in this helpful tool include:

- Female External Reproductive Organs

- Organs of the Female Reproductive System

- Anterior View of the Female Reproductive Organs

- Various Positions of the Uterus

- Layers of the Uterine Wall

- The Ovum from Fertilization Through Implantation

Activity 4.1: Those Helpful Hormones

Fill in the name of the hormone described below. (The first letter is provided to help you remember!)

1. H_____   A hormone secreted by the placenta whose presence in a woman's urine is the most
   C_____   common method of detecting pregnancy.
   G_____

2. P_____   A hormone secreted by the corpus luteum signaling the endometrium to develop in
   preparation for a zygote.

3. E_____   A hormone secreted by the ovaries whose level in the blood helps control the menstrual
   cycle.

4. P_____   A pituitary hormone that stimulates the production of milk from the mammary glands.

5. F_____-   A hormone secreted by the pituitary that instructs the ovaries to prepare an egg to be
   s_____   released by a follicle.
   hormone

6. L_____   A hormone secreted by the pituitary that stimulates ovulation.
   hormone

7. A_____   Male sex hormones.

8. T_____   The male sex hormone produced in the testes responsible for the development of male
   secondary sex characteristics.

Activity 4.2: A Different Look at Female Internal/External Anatomy

Using a plain manila file folder and magazine advertisement pictures, prepare a collage type replica of the female reproductive anatomy. External views should be on the outside of the folder, open the folder and create the internal view. Be sure to neatly and accurately label all the parts based on the terminology discussed in class and in your text book.

Activity 4.3: Breast Cancer Detection and Treatment

Explain the following concepts as they relate to breast cancer.

1. Breast self-exam

2. Clinical breast exam

3. Mammography

4. Needle biopsy

5. Open biopsy

6. Carcinoma

7. Metastasis

8. Lumpectomy

9. Mastectomy

10. Chemotherapy

11. Radiation therapy

12. Hormone therapy

Activity 4.4: 3-D Female Sexual Anatomy and Physiology

How might the following factors influence a woman's perceptions of her sexual anatomy and physiology?

Biological Factors and Female Sexual Anatomy and Physiology:

Psychological Factors and Female Sexual Anatomy and Physiology:

Sociocultural Factors and Female Sexual Anatomy and Physiology:

Want to know more? You can find additional information about topics covered in this chapter at sexuality.jbpub.com.

Chapter 5: Male Sexual Anatomy and Physiology

Learning Objectives

By the end of this chapter, you should be able to:

- Name and describe the parts of the male reproductive system to include the external and internal genitalia, including the pathway of the sperm.

- Discuss the role of hormones in males as they enter puberty.

- Cite various diseases that can affect the male reproductive system and the self-care procedures, as well as medical treatments associated with these diseases.

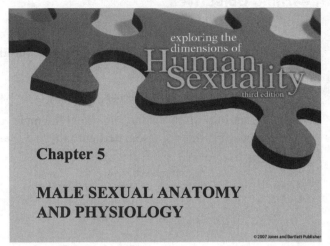

Chapter 5

MALE SEXUAL ANATOMY AND PHYSIOLOGY

© 2007 Jones and Bartlett Publisher

CHAPTER OBJECTIVES

- List and describe the internal and external male reproductive system.
- Discuss the role of hormones in males as they enter puberty.
- Cite various diseases that can affect the male reproductive system and their self-care procedures and treatments.

© 2007 Jones and Bartlett Publisher

THE MALE REPRODUCTIVE SYSTEM

- External genitals
- Male circumcision
- Internal genitals
- Pathway of the sperm

© 2007 Jones and Bartlett Publisher

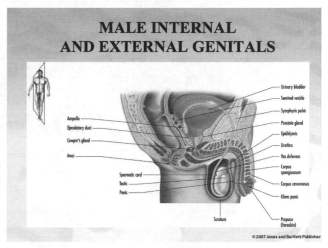

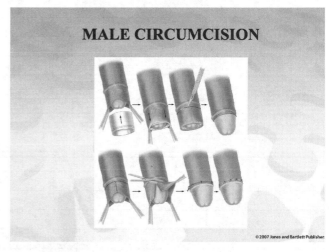

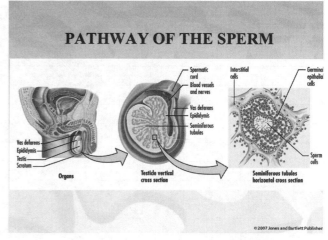

Notes

PATHWAY OF THE SPERM
(Continued)

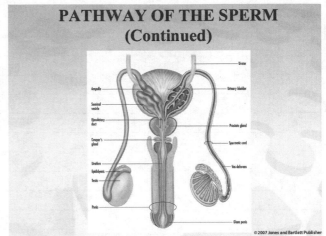

© 2007 Jones and Bartlett Publisher

HORMONES

- Male hormone function
  - Releasing factors
  - FSH and LH
  - Testosterone
- Male climacteric (male menopause)
  - Midlife crisis
- Hormone therapy
  - Testosterone supplements

© 2007 Jones and Bartlett Publisher

SELF-CARE AND PREVENTION

- Breast cancer in men
- The prostate
  - Prostate cancer (PSA)
  - Benign prostatic hyperplasia (BPH)
- Testicular cancer
  - Self-examine testicles

© 2007 Jones and Bartlett Publisher

MALES AND BIOLOGICAL FACTORS

- Chromosomes and genetics
- Physiological changes at puberty from testosterone
- Middle age: Testosterone levels drop—decreased muscle mass, increased fat, and reduced sex drive

© 2007 Jones and Bartlett Publisher

MALES AND PSYCHOLOGICAL FACTORS

- Body image and self-concept are enhanced for many men through exercise and sports.
- Men who suppress their emotions may increase levels of stress.
- Learned attitudes and behaviors about gender roles can lead to unhealthy lifestyles for men.

© 2007 Jones and Bartlett Publisher

MALES AND SOCIOCULTURAL FACTORS

- Laws affect conditions health insurance covers (Viagra).
- Religion—circumcision decision.
- Media and ads portray ideal man w/extreme muscularity, leading to distorted body image and maybe steroid use.
- Family, neighbors, friends reinforce gender stereotypes.

© 2007 Jones and Bartlett Publisher

Chapter 5 Summary: Fill in the Blanks

The Male Reproductive System

The male external genitals consist of the _____ and the scrotum. The penis contains the urethra, through which the ejaculate is emitted. Some penises have the foreskin (_____) intact, whereas others have had the foreskin surgically removed, a process called circumcision. The medical rationale for circumcision has varied over the years. The latest thinking is that circumcision may prevent urinary tract infections in male infants, as well as decrease the incidence of certain types of cancer in males and reproductive health problems in females. Circumcisions are also performed for religious and cultural reasons.

The male internal genitals contain numerous structures including the urethra, corpora _____, corpus _____, and the testes. It is the engorgement of blood in the corpora cavernosa and the corpus spongiosum during sexual stimulation that makes the penis erect. The testes are where sperm are produced (in the seminiferous tubules) and where testosterone is manufactured (in the interstitial cells).

Sperm are produced in the _____; are stored in the epididymis; travel up the _____; meet with secretions of the prostate, Cowper's glands, and seminal vesicles to form semen; and are ejaculated through the _____.

The endocrine glands most influencing sexual functions are the pituitary, which produces gonadotropins, and the adrenal glands, which produce androgens. The gonadotropins stimulate the testes to secrete progesterones, estrogens, and androgens.

Hormones

During puberty, boys become capable of _____. This is caused by the increased secretion of androgens, followed by the development of secondary sex characteristics. Accompanying male reproductive capacity, and also a result of increased androgen production, is a heightened interest in ____.

During puberty, increased _____ level leads to growth of the penis, prostate, seminal vesicles, and epididymis. Males cannot _____ before puberty because the prostate and seminal vesicles are not functional until they are "turned on" by the increased level of testosterone that emerge during puberty.

There is some evidence that men experience a climacteric as do women. Testosterone production lowers between the ages of _____ and _____ and can be accompanied by behavioral signs such as dating younger women and/or questioning sexual prowess. It is unclear whether these indications really identify a climacteric or if they are just part of the gradual process of aging. For example, the decrease in testosterone is so small that some experts consider it irrelevant.

Males are subjected to various reproductive-system illnesses and conditions. Among these are breast cancer, inflammation of the prostate (_____), enlargement of the prostate (_____), and prostate cancer. There are effective treatments for each of these conditions. However, treatments are most effective when the condition is diagnosed early. Hence the need for males to obtain regular medical screening and perform self-examinations.

Self-Care and Prevention

Breast cancer occurs in men, albeit rarely. Although treatment for men and women is the same, the psychological and emotional consequences of breast removal are not as significant for males as for females. _____ cancer is the second-leading cause of cancer death. Periodic physician exams can help screen for prostate cancer. Testicular cancer occurs most often in men aged _____ to _____. Monthly testicular self-exams can help catch the disease at an early stage, where treatment prognoses are good.

Focus on the Facts

Use the following table to help organize your review of the sexology researchers highlighted in this chapter.

Researchers	Type of research, findings, or statistics, and notes to help you remember.
External Genitals p. 170–175	
Internal Genitals p. 176–178	
Hormones p. 178–181	

Self-Care and Prevention
    Breast cancer & men
    Prostate
    Testes
    Penis
p. 181–185	

Test Your Knowledge. Are the Following Statements True or False?

Page numbers are provided to help you check your answers as you study.

1. True   False   Males can do Kegel exercises to strengthen muscles surrounding the penis. (p. 172)

2. True   False   Judaism and the Muslim faith require circumcision. (p. 173)

3. True   False   Sperm are produced in the Leydig cells of the testes. (p. 176)

4. True   False   There are approximately 30,000 sperm in each ejaculation. (p. 178)

5. True   False   Males may experience an increase in testosterone during between the ages of 40 to 50. (p. 180)

6. True   False   Internists or urologists are the medical professionals who specialize in male reproductive care. (p. 183)

7. True   False   Only females can have hormone therapy. (p. 180)

8. True   False   Prostatitis is the medical term for prostate cancer. (p. 181)

9. True   False   In a digital rectal exam, the health care provider inserts a finger into the rectum to check the prostate. (p. 182)

10. True   False   One risk factor for testicular cancer is undescended testes. (p. 184)

Learning anatomy and physiology, understanding the parts and how they function is complicated!

Are you confused yet? There are so many parts, inside and out, that many folks can't remember all the appropriate names. Some have never even seen all the parts. And what about the inside? Don't forget the web address that complements your text is designed to help you learn all these parts and how they function! Go to this site to find the interactive exercises to check your knowledge of the male reproductive system: **sexuality.jbpub.com.**

You will find:

- Male Reproductive Organs
- Posterior View of the Male Reproductive Organs
- Testicle Cross Section

Match the Following Male Reproductive Systems and Functions to the Appropriate Description.

a. Cowper's glands

b. Interstitial cells

c. Seminal vesicles

d. Prostatitis

e. Prostate gland

f. Corpus spongiosum

g. Spermatazoa

h. Corpora cavernosa

i. Vas deferens

j. Semen

k. Seminiferous tubules

l. Spermatic cord

m. Urethra

n. Epididymis

o. Ampulla

p. Testes

1. _____ Male gonads that produce sperm cells and male sex hormones.

2. _____ The cord from which the testicle is suspended that contains the vas deferens, blood vessels, nerves and muscle fibers.

3. _____ The tube through which the bladder empties urine outside the body and through which the male ejaculate exits.

4. _____ The mature male sperm cell.

5. _____ The male ejaculate which contains sperm and other secretions.

6. _____ A spongy body in the penis that contains a network of blood vessels and nerves.

7. _____ A structure of the male internal genitalia that secretes a fluid into semen before ejaculation to aid sperm motility and sperm life.

8. _____ A spongy body in the penis that contains a network of blood vessels and nerves.

9. _____ The duct through which sperm stored in the epididymis is passed, that is cut or blocked during vasectomy.

10. _____ Infection of the prostate gland.

11. _____ The structures located within the testes that actually produce the sperm.

12. _____ The cells (sometimes called the Leydig cells) between the seminiferous tubules where testosterone is produced.

13. _____ The enlarged portion of the vas deferens where sperm are provided nutrients from the seminal vesicles.

14. _____ The location where sperm are stored in the testes and where nutrients are provided to help the sperm develop.

15. _____ Two pea sized glands adjacent to the urethra that secrete a lubricating fluid before ejaculation.

16. _____ Two sacs of the male internal genitalia that secrete nutrients to nourish sperm.

Activity 5.1: Circumcision Decision

Identify the pros and cons of circumcision.

Pros: Cons:

If you have a son someday in the future, will you decide to have him circumcised or not? Why?

Activity 5.2: Testicular Examination

What are the risk factors for testicular cancer?

Testicular exam: what should males be looking for when examining their testes?

Activity 5.3: A Different Look at Male Internal/External Anatomy

Using a plain manila file folder and magazine advertisement pictures, prepare a collage type replica of the male reproductive anatomy. External views should be on the outside of the folder, open the folder and create the internal view. Be sure to neatly and accurately label all the parts based on the terminology discussed in class and in your text book.

Activity 5.4: 3-D Male Sexual Anatomy and Physiology

How might the following factors influence a man's perceptions of his sexual anatomy and physiology?

Biological Factors and Male Sexual Anatomy and Physiology:

Psychological Factors and Male Sexual Anatomy and Physiology:

Sociocultural Factors and Male Sexual Anatomy and Physiology:

Want to know more? You can find additional information about topics covered in this chapter at sexuality.jbpub.com.

Learning Objectives

By the end of this chapter, you should be able to:

- Discuss body image, its role in sexuality, and the way media have created impossible body-image ideals to emulate.

- Describe how to improve one's self-image.

- Describe the problems that poor body image causes for females and males, including eating disorders, muscle dysmorphia, steroid use, and cosmetic surgery.

Body Image Summary: Fill in the Blanks

Body image is the mental image we have of our own _____. People with a more positive body image are more likely to be open to sexual expression that exposes their body. The concept of the perfect body varies among people. It's important to make do with the genetic gifts we have rather than to try to be something we can never achieve.

A great deal of pre- and postproduction goes into the look of models and actors/actresses. The looks achieved are a vision of an art director rather than of reality. The mass media influences how adolescents believe they should look. The greater the frequency that adolescent girls read fashion magazines, the higher are unrealistic body expectations; in turn, the greater the chances of dieting and exercising to try to achieve those looks. People from diverse cultures often have very different ideals of beauty than those of mainstream American culture.

Building a Better Self-Image

Although few believe that their bodies are perfect, there are many things that can be done to improve one's body image.

Build on your given genetics. You can achieve a more optimal body weight through _____ and long-term changes in _____ habits.

Issues Related to Trying To Be Perfect

Issues relating to attempting perfection include eating disorders, steroid abuse, muscle dysmorphia, and cosmetic surgery. Anorexia nervosa and bulimia nervosa are _____ _____. Anorexia is a condition in which the individual severely limits calorie intake to achieve a thinner appearance. Bulimia is a condition in which the individual periodically _____ and _____ out of an obsessive fear of being fat.

Muscle dysmorphia is a condition in which an individual believes himself or herself to have _____, regardless of how muscular the person really is. Anabolic steroids are synthetic versions of _____. Abuse is widespread among adolescents, both to enhance athletic performance and improve appearance. Steroid use for nonmedical reasons is illegal, and can lead to many side-effects. Cosmetic ("plastic") surgery, liposuction, and breast implants are all surgical methods of changing physical appearance. Such procedures are expensive, and have potential side effects.

Focus on the Facts

Use the following table to help organize your review of the body image research highlighted in this chapter.

Topics	Type of research, findings, or statistics, and notes to help you remember.
Body Image *Perfect body?* *Perfect model?* *Media influence* *Diversity* p. 193–199	
Building Better Self-Image *Your body weight* *Diet* *Exercise* p. 199–202	
Disorders *Anorexia* *Bulimia* *Muscle dysmorphia* *Steroid use* p. 202–208	
Makeovers and Cosmetic Surgery p. 208–211	

Match the Following Definitions to the Appropriate Body Image Concepts.

a. Body mass index

b. Rhinoplasty

c. Bulimia nervosa

d. Liposuction

e. Steroids

f. Binge-eating disorder

g. Body image

h. Body composition

i. Cosmetic surgery

j. Muscle dysmorphia

k. Tummy tuck

l. Anorexia nervosa

1. _____ The mental image we have of our own physical appearance.

2. _____ Weight in kilogram divided by the square of the height in meters.

3. _____ Extensive surgical procedure that removes excess skin and fat from the abdomen.

4. _____ A condition in which the individual severely limits caloric intake.

5. _____ A condition in which the individual periodically binges and purges with an obsessive fear of becoming fat.

6. _____ Surgery done for the sole purpose of improving the appearance.

7. _____ A disorder whereby a bodybuilder in top shape considers him/herself to be puny.

8. _____ Synthetic versions of the male hormone testosterone that promote tissue growth.

9. _____ A technique for removing adipose tissue with a suction-pump device.

10. _____ Eating disorder characterized by recurrent binge eating but not by inappropriate weight control behaviors.

11. _____ Surgery done to change the shape of the nose.

12. _____ The percentage of fat versus lean tissue.

Activity IF.1 Body Image

Explain the following concepts as they are related to body image:

Eating disorders

Anorexia nervosa

Body dysmorphia

Adonis complex

Cosmetic surgery

Body piercing and tattoos

Want to know more? You can find additional information about topics covered in this chapter at sexuality.jbpub.com.

Learning Objectives

By the end of this chapter, you should be able to:

- Describe the biological, psychological, and sociocultural differences between males and females.

- Explain the effects of gender identity, gender roles, and sex stereotypes on sexuality.

- Analyze how the women's movement has affected both females and males.

Chapter 6

GENDER DIMENSIONS

© 2007 Jones and Bartlett Publishers

CHAPTER OBJECTIVES

- Describe the biological, psychological, and sociocultural differences between males and females.
- Explain the effects of gender identity, sex roles, and sex stereotypes on sexuality.
- Analyze how the women's movement has affected both males and females.

© 2007 Jones and Bartlett Publishers

GENDER DIFFERENCES

- Developmental differences
- Sex and abilities
- Sex and aggression
- Sex and health

© 2007 Jones and Bartlett Publishers

BIOLOGICAL FACTORS

- XX or XY chromosomes
  - X chromosomes are larger than Y and can supply the female with greater variety of genetic material
- Pubertal changes
  - Onset of puberty occurs approximately 2 years earlier in females
- Hormones and health

© 2007 Jones and Bartlett Publisher

PSYCHOLOGICAL FACTORS

- Expressiveness and communication differences
- Body image and self-esteem
- Different opportunities, motivation, and possibility of achievement

© 2007 Jones and Bartlett Publisher

SOCIOCULTURAL FACTORS

- Sex-role orientation begins at birth.
  - Children treated differently according to social standards for gender.
- People influence our thinking about gender by their actions.
- Ethnic groups have sex-specific heritage and sex roles.
- Mass media often sex-biased.

© 2007 Jones and Bartlett Publisher

GENDER DIFFERENCES

- Sex and dating
- Gender and the workplace
- Sex and advertising
- Myths about male-female differences
  - "Naturally" masculine or feminine
  - Real or apparent differences in behavior

©2007 Jones and Bartlett Publisher

GENDER IDENTITY, ROLES, AND STEREOTYPES

- Gender identity
- Teaching gender roles and stereotypes
  - Influence of school
  - Influence of parents and peers

© Dan Thomas Brostrom/ShutterStock, Inc.

©2007 Jones and Bartlett Publisher

GENDER IDENTITY, ROLES, AND STEREOTYPES

- Gender identity difficulty
  - Transsexualism
  - Gender reassignment
  - Gender dysphoria
- Influence of gender stereotypes on sexuality
  - Socialization
  - Communication styles
  - Intimacy
- Possibilities of androgyny

©2007 Jones and Bartlett Publisher

IN OTHERS' WORDS...

- "The condition of women affords in all countries the best criterion by which to judge the character of men."

  —*Frances Wright (1759–1852)*
  Views of Society and Manners in America, 1982

THE WOMEN'S MOVEMENT

- Gender equity
- Greater economic independence
- Greater control over reproduction
- Greater freedom from domination of males

Chapter 6 Summary: Fill in the Blanks

Gender Differences

Gender differences are determined biologically, psychologically, and socioculturally. Biology alone does not determine any individual's interests, abilities, or relationships. There are gender differences in development. Females are more developed at birth, but boys develop more rapidly after birth. The onset of puberty is about _____ years earlier in females. Although some differences in abilities have been observed between genders, the differences are slight. At age 11 or 12, females have greater abilities in language and verbal tasks, whereas males perform better in _____ _____ tasks. Males are more aggressive than females.

Further differences exist in health: women live longer than men, but experience more health problems. The media aspect of the sociocultural dimension contributes to our thinking about femininity and masculinity. MTV videos tend to be stereotyped. Ads with voice-overs use the male voice in 90% of ads.

Gender, Identity, and Stereotypes

Gender identity is a function of biology (both function and appearance), psychology (how you feel about your gender), and gender socialization. Gender identity is the awareness and acceptance of one's gender. Gender typing is the process by which children develop behavior appropriate to their gender. Gender _____ is the concept that people's genders do not change—even if they change their actions or clothing. Gender _____ is a grouping of mental representations about male and female physical qualities, behaviors, and personality traits.

Gender roles are taught throughout the life cycle, but parents have a strong impact on their children. With a mother at home more often, girls have a gender role model to follow; yet boys typically do not. Even in two-income families, mothers still do more housework and childrearing than fathers. Schools also reinforce stereotypes through their differing treatment of children of different genders. Gender _____ is the feeling of being trapped in the body of the wrong gender. A _____ is a person whose gender identity does not match his or her biological gender. The term also refers to persons who wish to have—or have had—gender reassignment surgery (having their genitals surgically altered to conform to their gender identity).

Gender stereotypes limit self-expression and personal growth and development—in turn, impacting sexuality. Social pressure to conform to gender stereotypes creates anxieties. Androgynous people exhibit a combination of _____ and _____ traits as defined by society. The idea of androgyny does away with gender-role stereotypes.

The Women's Movement

The women's movement has allowed women a greater freedom to explore their potential. Women have achieved greater economic independence, greater control over reproduction, and greater freedom from the domination of males. Although many gender-based biases still exist for women, the women's movement has brought important socially based gender issues to the forefront and allowed a forum to debate such issues.

Focus on the Facts

Use the following table to help organize your review of the gender researchers highlighted in this chapter.

Topic	Type of research, findings, or statistics, and notes to help you remember.
Gender Differences *Developmental* *Abilities* *Aggression* *Health* *Dating* *Workplace* p. 218–231	
Gender Identity, Roles & Stereotypes *Influence of schools* *Influence of* *parents & peers* p. 232–240	
Transsexualism p. 240–243	
Androgyny p. 246–247	
Women's Movement p. 247–251	

Match the Following Gender Concepts with the Appropriate Definitions

a. Gender constancy

b. Gender dysphoria

c. Gender-role stereotyping

d. Gender typing

e. Gender role

f. Gender schema

g. Gender identity

h. Oedipus complex

1. _____ Complex groups of ways males and females are expected to behave in a given culture.

2. _____ A developmental stage in which the boys wants to possess his mother sexually and sees the father as a rival.

3. _____ Feeling trapped in the body of the "wrong" sex.

4. _____ The process whereby children develop behavior that is appropriate to their gender.

5. _____ The concept that people's genders do not change, even if they change their dress or behavior.

6. _____ A grouping of mental representations about male and female physical qualities, behaviors, and personality traits.

7. _____ The awareness and acceptance of one's gender.

8. _____ Expectation that individuals will behavior in certain ways because they are male or female.

Test Your Knowledge. Are the following Statements True or False?

Page numbers are provided to help you check your answers as you study.

1. True   False   Males tend to have higher visual spatial skills and females tend to have greater abilities in language and verbal tasks. (p. 220)

2. True   False   According to Tavris, boys resort to physical aggression, girls to "relational" aggression. (p. 222)

3. True   False   Males die an average of 10 years earlier than women. (p. 225)

4. True   False   In 2003 the typical male worker received $176 for every $100 earned by a female (p. 231)

5. True   False   Psychoanalytic theory as explained by Freud describes gender typing as boys identify with their fathers and girls with their mothers. (p. 232)

6. True   False   Gender-role stereotyping is one's self-image as a female or male. (p. 234)

7. True   False   Teachers never treat boys and girls differently. (p. 236)

8. True   False   Transsexuals do not derive sexual excitement from cross-dressing. (p. 240)

9. True   False   Androgyny allows males and females to express feelings without the confining demands of gender-role stereotypes. (p. 246)

10. True   False   Social and economic inequities between the sexes still exist. (p. 249)

Activity 6.1: Shaping Your Gender

How has your experience in school shaped your gender role and your personal expectations?

Who has had the greatest influence on your gender identity? Why?

Activity 6.2: Media Gender Analysis

Find and attach an article, cartoon, or advertisement that conveys a gender message. Analyze the media portrayal of gender. Answer the following questions:

What is the message?

What examples are used to convey this message?

Does the message fit a gender-role stereotype? Why?

Is the gender message consistent with your beliefs about gender?

How do you think this message would fit your parent's expectations of gender role? Why?

Activity 6.3: 3-D Gender

Describe how the following factors influence how you perceive the world and express yourself as a male or female.

Biological Factors and Your Gender:

Psychological Factors and Your Gender:

Sociocultural Factors and Your Gender:

Want to know more? You can find additional information about topics covered in this chapter at sexuality.jbpub.com.

Chapter 7: Sexual Response and Arousal

Learning Objectives

By the end of this chapter, you should be able to:

- Describe the role of the brain in sexual response, including the hormones involved and the role they play.

- Describe the four phases of the Masters and Johnson sexual response cycle, as well as other theoretical models of sexual response.

- Describe the physiology of orgasm in both males and females, differentiating between the different types of orgasm.

Notes

_____
_____
_____
_____
_____
_____
_____
_____
_____
_____
_____
_____
_____
_____
_____
_____
_____
_____
_____
_____
_____
_____
_____
_____
_____
_____
_____
_____
_____
_____
_____
_____
_____
_____
_____
_____
_____

exploring the
dimensions of
Human
Sexuality
third edition

Chapter 7

SEXUAL RESPONSE AND AROUSAL

©2007 Jones and Bartlett Publishers

CHAPTER OBJECTIVES

- Describe the role of the brain in sexual response, including the hormones involved and the roles they play.
- Describe the Masters & Johnson sexual response cycle and other theoretical models of sexual response.
- Describe the physiology of orgasm in both males and females, differentiating between the various types of orgasm.

©2007 Jones and Bartlett Publishers

HOW THE MIND AND BODY CONTROL SEXUAL RESPONSE

- The brain: master of the body
  - Interprets stimulation
  - Cerebral cortex
  - Limbic system
  - Reticular activating system
- The brain and sexual response
  - Variation in sexual response even though brain reactions to stimuli are typical

©2007 Jones and Bartlett Publishers

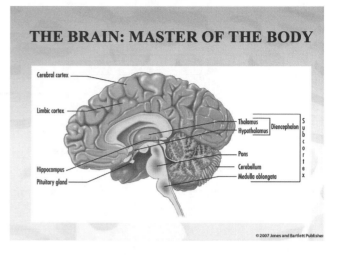

THE BRAIN: MASTER OF THE BODY

Cerebral cortex
Limbic cortex
Thalamus
Hypothalamus
Diencephalon
Subcortex
Pons
Cerebellum
Hippocampus
Medulla oblongata
Pituitary gland

© 2007 Jones and Bartlett Publisher

THE BRAIN AND SEXUAL RESPONSE—THE 5 SENSES

- Seeing
- Hearing
- Touching
- Smelling
- Tasting

© 2007 Jones and Bartlett Publisher

HOW THE MIND AND BODY CONTROL SEXUAL RESPONSE

- Autonomic nervous system
- Role of hormones in sexual arousal
- Aphrodisiacs

© 2007 Jones and Bartlett Publisher

Notes

_____
_____
_____
_____
_____
_____
_____
_____
_____
_____
_____
_____
_____
_____
_____
_____
_____
_____
_____
_____
_____
_____
_____
_____
_____
_____
_____
_____
_____
_____
_____
_____
_____
_____
_____

IN OTHERS' WORDS…

- Shakespeare's Macbeth on alcohol and sexual response:

"Provokes the desire, but takes away the performance!"

© 2007 Jones and Bartlett Publishers

THE MASTERS & JOHNSON SEXUAL RESPONSE CYCLE

- Excitement phase
- Plateau phase
- Orgasm phase (emission and expulsion)
- Resolution phase (refractory)

© 2007 Jones and Bartlett Publishers

MALE   FEMALE

(a) Phase of Sexual Response Cycle

(b) Phase of Sexual Response Cycle

© 2007 Jones and Bartlett Publishers

OTHER THEORETICAL MODELS OF SEXUAL RESPONSE

- Kaplan's triphasic model
  - Desire, excitement, resolution
- Zilbergeld and Ellison's model
  - Interest or desire, arousal, physiological readiness, orgasm, satisfaction

© 2007 Jones and Bartlett Publishers

ORGASM

- Reed's erotic stimulus pathway:
  - Seduction phase (memories and rituals)
  - Sensations phase (extension of plateau phase)
  - Surrender phase ("psycho-physiological surprise" of orgasm)
  - Reflection phase (evaluating the experience)
- Types of orgasm:
  - Vulval orgasm (not sexually satiating)
  - Uterine orgasm (sexually satiating)
  - Blended orgasm
- Controversies about orgasm

© 2007 Jones and Bartlett Publishers

SEXUAL RESPONSE CURVE

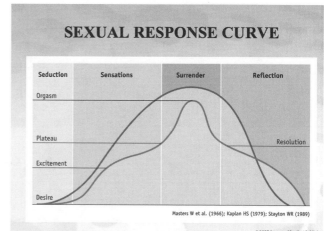

Masters W et al. (1966); Kaplan HS (1979); Stayton WR (1989)

© 2007 Jones and Bartlett Publishers

SEXUAL RESPONSE AND AROUSAL: BIOLOGICAL FACTORS

- Physiological reactions to sexual stimuli.
- Masters and Johnson showed differences between males and females.
- Body releases hormones when sexually stimulated.
- Physical disabilities, injuries, alcohol, drugs, or illness may affect sexual response.

© 2007 Jones and Bartlett Publisher

SEXUAL RESPONSE AND AROUSAL: PSYCHOLOGICAL FACTORS

- Feelings toward partner influence sexual response derived.
- Level of experience influences our response to sexual stimuli.
- Learned attitudes and behaviors include discovering stimuli to which we respond.
- Body image influences self-concept.

© 2007 Jones and Bartlett Publisher

SEXUAL RESPONSE AND AROUSAL: SOCIOCULTURAL FACTORS

- Religious beliefs influence our feelings about sexuality in general.
- Culture and ethnic heritage influence what we find sensual or attractive.
- Media/ads influence types of stimulation we react to.
- Ethical decisions guide sexual behaviors leading to arousal.

© 2007 Jones and Bartlett Publisher

Chapter 7 Summary: Fill in the Blanks

Sexual Arousal and Response

The brain is the key player in sexual arousal. When a sexual stimulus is encountered (sight, touch, smell, sound), the message is passed via nerves to the brain. Upon reaching the brain, these messages pass through the _____ _____ either from or to the limbic system and the thalamus. The limbic system is where emotion evolves, and the thalamus serves as the switchboard, determining what to do with incoming messages. Next, the hypothalamus is activated, which in turn activates the autonomic nervous system and the endocrine system through messages sent via nerves or substances released into the bloodstream. No two people respond the same way to sexual stimulation. What turns one person on may turn another person off.

Hormones control sexual response to a given stimulus. Sexual hormones are produced in the _____ and _____. Testosterone affects sexual interest, or libido. Artificial steroid hormones, like Androstenedione, may not provide sexual benefits and may have harmful side effects. Aphrodisiacs are any substances that arouse sexual desire and/or enhance sexual response. Most do not work as promised and have potentially serious side effects. Anaphrodisiacs are substances that inhibit sexual desire.

The Masters and Johnson Sexual Response Cycle

Masters and Johnson described the human sexual response as consisting of four phases: _____, plateau, orgasm, and resolution. Many nongenital physical changes accompany sexual arousal; for example, the nipples become erect, the skin flushes, muscles tense, breathing speeds up, the heart beats faster, and blood pressure rises.

Genital changes also occur as a result of sexual arousal; for example, blood vessels become congested, the clitoris or the penis become erect, the vagina becomes wet, and Bartholin's glands (female) and Cowper's glands (male) secrete a few drops of fluid. The female sexual response is more varied than the male's. Males generally move from excitement to plateau to orgasm and then to resolution. They can experience another orgasm but only after a _____ (recovery) period. Females sometimes experience a sexual response cycle similar to that of males except they can have multiple orgasms without a refractory period. In addition, females can move from the excitement phase to plateau and, without having an orgasm, return to resolution; or they can experience rapid escalation from excitement to orgasm without experiencing a definitive plateau phase.

Other models of the human sexual response have been presented. For example, Kaplan described sexual response as consisting of three phases (triphasic model): _____, excitement, and resolution. Zilbergeld and Ellison described sexual response in their five-component model. The components in this model are interest (or desire), arousal, physiological readiness, orgasm, and _____. David Reed describes the sexual response to include four phases: seduction, sensation, _____, and reflection.

Orgasm

Orgasm is the release of sexual tension resulting in muscular contractions and ejaculation (at least in males). In males it is generally followed by a refractory period in which orgasm is not possible. In females, orgasm can occur without a refractory period. For either gender, if there is no second orgasm, the body enters the resolution phase, during which the body's physiology _____. Orgasm in females is preceded by the uterus increasing in size and elevating, the inner two-thirds of the vagina lengthening and expanding (sometimes called tenting), lubrication of the vaginal walls, engorgement of blood in the outer third of the vagina to form an _____ _____, and retraction of the clitoris under the clitoral hood.

In males, orgasm is a two-stage process: emission and expulsion. Emission involves contractions of the vas deferens, the seminal vesicles, the prostate, and the external and internal urethral sphincters. Expulsion consists of a relaxing of the external urethral sphincter, contractions of the urethra and the muscles at the base of the penis and the anus, and the expelling of the ejaculate from the penis.

Orgasms vary from person to person and from orgasm to orgasm within the same person. Sexual pleasure can be obtained without an orgasm and, in fact, striving for an orgasm (having it as the goal of the sexual encounter) may even interfere with sexual satisfaction. Simultaneous orgasm is undeniably an exciting event when it occurs, but it is only one of a wide range of satisfying sexual patterns. Setting it up as a goal can be dysfunctional.

Focus on the Facts

Use the following table to help organize your review of the sexual response and arousal researchers highlighted in this chapter.

Researchers	Stages of sexual response and brief description of what happens in each stage.		
	Stage	Male	Female
Masters and Johnson p. 261–267			
Kaplan p. 267–268			

Researchers	Stages of sexual response and brief description of what happens in each stage.		
	Stage	Male	Female
Zilbergeld and Ellison p. 268			
Walen and Roth p. 269			
Thayton p. 269			
Basson p. 269			
Reed p. 270–271			

Test Your Knowledge. Are the Following Statements True or False?

Page numbers are provided to help you check your answers as you study.

1. True   False   The reticular activating system (RAS) only sends psychological messages from the brain to the body. (p. 259)

2. True   False   Testosterone affects sexual interest or libido. (p. 260)

3. True   False   Aphrodisiacs are guaranteed to enhance sexual arousal and orgasm. (p. 271)

4. True   False   Sex flush is more common in males. (p. 263)

5. True   False   Transudation is the process resulting in vaginal lubrication. (p. 262)

6. True   False   Orgasms always feel the same. (p. 264)

7. True   False   In the refractory period, a male is able to have another erection right after an ejaculation. (p. 264)

8. True   False   Kaplan's model of sexual response includes a psychological prephysical stage of desire. (p. 268)

9. True   False   In Reed's model of sexual response, the reflection phase allows for interpretation of the sexual experience. (p. 271)

10. True   False   You cannot fake an orgasm. (p. 276)

Fill in the Correct Term for the Following Definitions:

p. 258

1. The part of the brain called the gray matter that controls higher order functioning such as language and judgment. _____

2. The part of the brain referred to as the sea of emotion which produces emotions in response to physical and psychological signals. _____

3. A network of nerves that connect the cortex and the subcortex—the connection between mind and body. _____

p. 261

4. The sequence of physiological and psychological reactions as a result of sexual arousal. _____

5. The process of vaginal lubrication resulting from engorgement of blood that creates pressure that forces moisture to seep from the spaces between the cells. _____

p. 262

6. The valve the prevents urine from entering the urethra and sperm from entering the bladder during ejaculation. _____

7. The valve that closes during the emission stage, resulting in a buildup of semen, and that opens during the ejaculation stage, allowing the semen to be expelled. _____

8. A darkening of the skin of the neck, face, forehead, or chest during sexual stimulation. _____

9. Muscle tension occurring during sexual arousal. _____

10. Deep and rapid breathing that occurs during sexual excitation. _____

11. An increase in heart rate that occurs during sexual activity. _____

12. Increased blood flow to the area of the body which occurs in the pelvic area during sexual arousal. _____

p. 264

13. The narrowing of the outer third of the vagina during orgasm caused by contractions of the muscles in that area. _____

14. The time needed by males for recovery between orgasms. _____

15. Orgasms that occur without the need for a refractory or recovery period. _____

p. 268

16. The first stage of the response cycle as described by Kaplan's model which consists of psychologically becoming interested in sex before any physical changes occur.

_____

17. The second stage of Kaplan's model which consists of physiological arousal and changes and possibly orgasm. _____

18. The stage of the sexual response cycle consisting of a return to the non-aroused state.

_____

p. 276

19. Surgical removal of the clitoris. _____

20. An orgasm in a female that includes the contractions of the orgasmic platform which is not sexually satisfying and, as a result, allows another orgasm to occur almost immediately.

_____

21. An orgasm in a female in which there are contractions of the muscles in the outer third of the vagina as well as breath holding; a combination of the vulva and uterine orgasms.

_____

Quick Question

What similarities and differences are seen in the sexual response cycles of males and females?

Masters and Johnson Stage	Male	Both	Female
Excitement			
Plateau			
Orgasm			
Resolution			

Chapter 8: Contraception

Learning Objectives

By the end of this chapter, you should be able to:

- Discuss the reasons to use contraceptives, how to choose a contraceptive, and the difference between perfect use and typical use.

- Evaluate the nonprescription methods of contraception, including the effectiveness, the reversibility, and the advantages and disadvantages of each. Explain why some have higher rates of user effectiveness than others.

- Evaluate the prescription methods of contraception, including the effectiveness, the reversibility, and the advantages and disadvantages of each. Explain why some have higher rates of user effectiveness than others.

- Discuss the viability of future contraceptive methods. Consider the impact of gender issues, pharmaceutical industry costs for litigation, federal regulation compliance, and FDA approval. (p. 257)

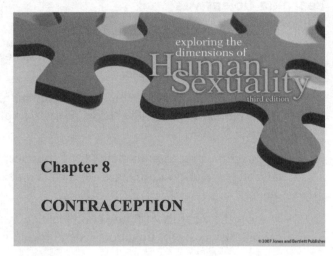

Chapter 8

CONTRACEPTION

©2007 Jones and Bartlett Publishers

CHAPTER OBJECTIVES

- Discuss the reasons to use contraceptives, ways to choose a contraceptive, and the difference between perfect use and typical use.
- Evaluate the nonprescription methods of contraception, including the effectiveness, the reversibility, and the advantages and disadvantages of each. Explain why some have higher rates of user effectiveness than others.

©2007 Jones and Bartlett Publishers

CHAPTER OBJECTIVES

- Evaluate the prescription methods of contraception, including the effectiveness, the reversibility, and the advantages and disadvantages of each. Explain why some have higher rates of user effectiveness than others.
- Discuss the viability of future contraceptive methods. Consider the impact of gender issues, pharmaceutical industry costs for litigation, federal regulation compliance, and FDA approval.

©2007 Jones and Bartlett Publishers

IN OTHERS' WORDS...

- "No woman can call herself free who does not own and control her body. No woman can call herself free until she can choose consciously whether she will or will not be a mother."

  – *Margaret Sanger*

© 2007 Jones and Bartlett Publishers

METHOD EFFECTIVENESS

The difference between perfect use and typical use is an indication of how much human error may influence the contraceptive.

- Perfect use
  - The ability of a method of contraception to prevent pregnancy as measured by consistent and correct use
- Typical use
  - The ability of a method of contraception to prevent pregnancy as actually used at home by people not being monitored

© 2007 Jones and Bartlett Publishers

CONTRACEPTION

- Contraception versus safer sex
  - Many effective contraceptives provide no protection from sexually transmitted infections.
- Deciding to use contraception

© Jones and Bartlett Publishers. Photographed by Christine McKeen   © 2007 Jones and Bartlett Publishers

Notes

_____

_____

_____

_____

_____

_____

_____

_____

_____

_____

_____

_____

_____

_____

_____

_____

_____

_____

_____

_____

_____

_____

_____

_____

_____

_____

_____

_____

_____

_____

_____

_____

_____

_____

_____

ABSTINENCE

- Abstinence
  - Effectiveness (no data to compare)
  - Reversibility (complete and immediate)
  - Advantages (free, no side effects, nothing to remember)
  - Disadvantages (must be used every time; requires strong self-control and commitment)

© 2007 Jones and Bartlett Publishers

WITHDRAWAL

- Withdrawal
  - Effectiveness (73%–96%)
  - Reversibility (complete and immediate)
  - Advantages (free, available, ease of use, no side effects, encourages male involvement)
  - Disadvantages (possibility of failing to recognize impending ejaculation, interrupts sexual pleasure, great self-control required on the part of the male, relatively high failure rate)

© 2007 Jones and Bartlett Publishers

NONPRESCRIPTION METHODS

- Male condom
  - Consistent use
  - Correct use
  - Effectiveness (85%–98%)
  - Advantages
  - Disadvantages
  - Communication dimensions
  - Multicultural dimensions
  - *Check expiration date; don't keep them in the car or wallet; don't use w/petroleum-based products.*

Photographed by Kimberly Potvin

© 2007 Jones and Bartlett Publishers

Notes

NONPRESCRIPTION METHODS

- Female condom
  - Effectiveness (79%–95%)
  - Advantages
  - Disadvantages

Photographed by Kimberly Potvin

© 2007 Jones and Bartlett Publishers

NONPRESCRIPTION METHODS

- Spermicides
  - Effectiveness (71%–85%)
  - Reversibility (complete and immediate)
  - Advantages
  - Disadvantages

Photographed by Kimberly Potvin

© 2007 Jones and Bartlett Publishers

NATURAL FAMILY PLANNING

- Fertility awareness methods
  - Calendar method
  - Ovulation method
    - Basal body temperature
    - Cervical secretions
  - Sympto-thermal method
    - Effectiveness (91%–99% if practiced perfectly)
    - Reversibility (complete and immediate)
    - Advantages

© 2007 Jones and Bartlett Publishers

Notes

_____

_____

_____

_____

_____

_____

_____

_____

_____

_____

_____

_____

_____

_____

_____

_____

_____

_____

_____

_____

_____

_____

_____

_____

_____

_____

_____

_____

_____

_____

_____

_____

_____

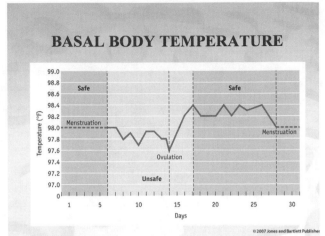

BASAL BODY TEMPERATURE

PRESCRIPTION METHODS: ORAL CONTRACEPTIVES

- Combination pill
- Effectiveness (95%–99.9%)
- Reversibility

- Advantages
- Disadvantages
- Emergency contraception

Photographed by Kimberly Potvin

© 2007 Jones and Bartlett Publisher

CONTRACEPTIVE PATCH

- Effectiveness (92%–99.7%)
- Reversibility
- Advantages
  - Convenient

- Disadvantages
  - 20% of users experience side effects

Photographed by Kimberly Potvin

© 2007 Jones and Bartlett Publisher

PRESCRIPTION METHODS:
DEPO-PROVERA

- Effectiveness (99.7%)
- Reversibility
- Advantages
- Disadvantages

© 2007 Jones and Bartlett Publishers

PRESCRIPTION METHODS:
INTRAUTERINE DEVICES (IUDs)

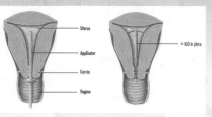

- Effectiveness (99%)
- Reversibility
- Advantages/disadvantages

© 2007 Jones and Bartlett Publishers

PRESCRIPTION METHODS:
DIAPHRAGM

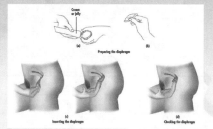

- Effectiveness (84%–94%)
- Reversibility
- Advantages
- Disadvantages

© 2007 Jones and Bartlett Publishers

PRESCRIPTION METHODS: CERVICAL CAP

- Effectiveness (84%–91%)
- Reversibility
- Advantages
- Disadvantages

Photographed by Kimberly Potvin

© 2007 Jones and Bartlett Publisher

NUVARING

- Vaginal birth control
  - Provides hormonal protection from pregnancy
  - Approved by FDA in 2001

Photographed by Kimberly Potvin   © 2007 Jones and Bartlett Publisher

PERMANENT METHODS: STERILIZATION

- Effectiveness (nearly 100%)
- Reversibility
- Advantages
  - Permanent
  - Highly effective
- Disadvantages
  - Provides no protection against STIs

© 2007 Jones and Bartlett Publisher

MALE STERILIZATION

- Vasectomy
- Reversibility through vasovasectomy

FEMALE STERILIZATION

- Minilaparotomy
- Laparoscopy
- Open laparoscopy
- Vaginal approaches
- Transcervical methods
- Reversibility

THE FUTURE OF CONTRACEPTIVES

- Male contraceptive implants
- New implants: Implanon, Jadelle
- Cervical cap: Lea's Shield
- Sterilization: Essure

BIOLOGICAL FACTORS INFLUENCING CONTRACEPTION

- Gender
  - Males: condoms or vasectomy
  - Females: only they can become pregnant
- Not all protect against STIs
- NFP relies on physiological markers to monitor ovulation
- Hormones

©2007 Jones and Bartlett Publisher

PSYCHOLOGICAL FACTORS INFLUENCING CONTRACEPTION

- Experience may determine contraceptive you choose.
- Emotions often get in the way of practicing contraception and safer sex.
- Learned attitudes and behaviors affect your willingness to negotiate contraceptive use and practice safer sex.
- Your self-concept may influence your contraceptive behaviors.

©2007 Jones and Bartlett Publisher

SOCIOCULTURAL FACTORS INFLUENCING CONTRACEPTION

- Socioecomonic status affects availability and use of contraceptives.
- Laws and government regulations limit contraceptive approval and availability.
- Religion affects contraceptive decisions.
- Media and ad information can affect both contraceptive choice and brand choice.

©2007 Jones and Bartlett Publisher

Chapter 8 Summary: Fill in the Blanks

Contraception

There is no perfect, foolproof method of contraception. When choosing a method, considerations include the effectiveness, side effects, convenience, cost, and STI/HIV protection as well as the partner's agreement to use it each and every time. Perfect use is the ability of a method of contraception to prevent pregnancy as measured by

_____. Typical use is the ability of a method of contraception to prevent pregnancy as actually used at home by people not being monitored.

Methods of contraception should not be confused with prevention of STIs/HIV. Most contraceptive methods provide no protection from STIs/HIV; in fact, the IUD actually increases the likelihood of STIs. Three ways to achieve effectiveness against pregnancy and disease transmission are abstinence, use of latex or polyurethane condoms and a spermicide together, or use of latex or polyurethane condoms and a hormonal contraceptive together.

Nonprescription Methods

Abstinence is the only _____% effective method of fertility control and STI prevention. Effective communication and commitment to the method are key to making it work. Withdrawal, or coitus interruptus, which involves the man withdrawing his penis from the vagina before ejaculation, offers no protection from STIs. Latex and polyurethane condoms are barrier methods of contraception and provide protection against STIs/HIV. The female condom is a loose-fitting polyurethane sheath with rings on either side. One ring covers the cervix, the other ring remains outside the vagina and partially covers the vulva.

Spermicides kill and/or immobilize sperm on contact and act as a cervical barrier (p. 299) , preventing movement toward an egg. Spermicides are available as (p. 299) foam, gels, films, suppositories, sponges, and tablets.

_____ methods (calendar method, ovulation method, and sympto-thermal method) are based on a woman identifying the days in her menstrual cycle when she is most likely to be fertile, and then avoiding intercourse during those days or using a barrier method or withdrawal during those days (fertility-awareness-combined methods).

Prescription Methods

Oral contraceptives (the Pill) refer to a daily pill to prevent ovulation. They can be categorized as sequential pills, combined pills (containing _____and _____), minipills (progestin-only), and multiphasic formulations. Emergency contraception is now available within 72 hours of unprotected intercourse. (The emergency contraceptive hotline is 1-888-NOT2-LATE.) The contraceptive patch delivers a combination of estrogen and progesterone through the skin.

A vaginal NuvaRing can be inserted in the vagina for 21 days. This ring contains estrogen and progestin and requires a prescription.

Intrauterine devices (IUDs) are synthetic devices that are inserted by a medical provider into the uterus to prevent pregnancy. The diaphragm prevents the sperm from traveling through the uterus and up the fallopian tubes to fertilize an egg, and it holds _____ against the cervix. It must be fitted by a trained provider. The cervical cap is a rubber, plastic, or metal cap that covers the cervix and holds spermicidal cream or jelly. It must be fitted by a trained provider.

Permanent Methods: Sterilization

Sterilization is a permanent method of contraception. More than 15 million Americans rely on sterilization as their primary method. In males, a vasectomy entails cutting or cauterizing the _____ to prevent sperm from being ejaculated. In females, sterilization can take several forms. In a minilaparotomy (or "minilap"), a small incision is made in the abdomen through which the fallopian tubes are brought so they can be blocked by ligation (the tying of the fallopian tubes to prevent sperm/egg union). In a laparoscopy, a laparoscope is inserted through an abdominal incision; then, a ligation is performed, or clips or rings are applied to block the fallopian tubes. An open laparoscopy combines the methods of the minilaparotomy and the laparotomy.

Two types of vaginal female sterilization are the culpotomy and the culdoscopy. With the success of the minilaparotomy and the laparotomy, the vaginal approaches are not often used. Although some sterilizations are reversible, all sterilizations should be considered permanent.

The Future of Contraceptives

Research on new contraceptives is ongoing. Some attempts include male contraceptive implants, Implanon progesterone implant, Jadelle two-rod implants, Lea's Shield cervical cap, and Essure nonsurgical sterilization.

Focus on the Facts

Use the following table to help organize your review of the contraceptive methods highlighted in this chapter.

Method	Prescription Required?	How it works	Advantages	Disadvantages
Abstinence				
Withdrawal				
Male Condom				
Female Condom				
Spermicides				
Natural Family Planning				
Oral Contraceptives				
Depo-provera or Lunelle Injections				

Method	Prescription Required?	How it works	Advantages	Disadvantages
Contraceptive Patch				
Intrauterine Devices (IUD)				
Diaphragm				
Cervical Cap				
Sterilization				
NuvaRing Vaginal Ring				

Test Your Knowledge. Are the Following Statements True or False?

Page numbers are provided to help you check your answers as you study.

1. True   False   The United States has a higher rate of unintended pregnancies than all other developed countries. (p. 288)

2. True   False   The effectiveness rate of perfect use is always higher than that of typical use. (p. 287)

3. True   False   Withdrawal is better than nothing if trying to prevent pregnancy. (p. 292)

4. True   False   Latex male condoms can be washed and reused. (p. 292)

5. True   False   Male and female condoms provide some protection from sexually transmitted disease. (p. 297)

6. True   False   Spermicides come in many different forms. (p. 299)

7. True   False   Sympto-thermal methods of natural family planning are as effective as most prescription contraceptives. (p. 300)

8. True   False   Even women who smoke can use the new brands of oral contraceptive pills. (p. 305)

9. True   False   Contraceptive patch users must apply a new patch daily. (p. 307)

10. True   False   Depo-Povera must be injected every month. (p. 307)

11. True   False   As of March 2003, there are no plans for Norplant to be reintroduced in the U.S. (p. 308)

12. True   False   The IUD is no longer available in the United States. (p. 308)

13. True   False   The diaphragm is a shallow rubber cap that holds spermicide against the cervix. (p. 308)

14. True   False   NuvaRing is difficult to insert correctly. (p. 311)

15. True   False   Sterilization is a form of contraception that renders a person biologically incapable of reproducing. (p. 314)

16. True   False   Female sterilization is called a vasectomy. (p. 315)

Review the Types of Contraceptive Methods:

Match the following to the appropriate **method or procedure** as described in your text.

a. Nonoxynol 9 (N-9)

b. Typical use

c. Coitus interruptus

d. Female condom

e. Fertility awareness methods

f. Calendar method

g. Natural family planning

h. Combined pill

i. Emergency contraception

j. Ovulation methods

k. Basal body temperature

l. Intrauterine devices and systems

m. Cervical cap

n. Minipill

o. Depo-Provera

p. Vasovasectomy

1. _____ Reversal of a vasectomy so that sperm can be ejaculated.

2. _____ Calculation of a woman's fertile times and abstention from intercourse on fertile days.

3. _____ The Latin term for withdrawal.

4. _____ A polyurethane sheath worn inside the vagina.

5. _____ An injectable progestin only contraceptive.

6. _____ The major spermicidal ingredient in U.S.-made products.

7. _____ Oral contraceptive containing estrogen and progestin.

8. _____ Methods used to determine fertile days.

9. _____ Charting the length of a woman's periods for several months to determine the days she is most likely to be fertile.

10. _____ Observation of the signs of ovulation to calculate fertile days.

11. _____ A woman's body temperature immediately upon waking.

12. _____ Synthetic device that is inserted into the uterus to prevent the sperm from fertilizing the ovum.

13. _____ A progestin only contraceptive pill.

14. _____ The use of oral contraceptives after unprotected sex has occurred mid-cycle.

15. _____ Shallow rubber cap smaller than a diaphragm that covers the cervix to prevent sperm from entering the uterus.

16. _____ The ability of a contraception to prevent pregnancy as actually used at home by people not being monitored.

Activity 8.1: Contraception in the Real World

What is the difference between a contraceptive's perfect use and its typical use?

What factors may influence the difference between the theoretical effectiveness and user effectiveness of contraceptives?

Explain how the following methods of natural family planning are used: (p. 300–302)

Calendar method-

Ovulation methods-

Basal body temperature-

Cervical secretions-

Sympto-thermal method-

What type of couple would be successful using natural family planning methods?

Activity 8.2: WEB-EX

Access the *Interactive Program to Help You Choose the Birth Control Method That's Right for You* through the "Want to know more?" section on the text web site below or at *www.arhp.org/patienteducation/interactivetools/choosing/index.cfm?ID=275*

Based on your answers, a recommendation for contraceptives that may best fit your medical profile and lifestyle choices will be provided. Remember, there is no "best method" of birth control. Each has advantages and disadvantages. And the method that best suits you now may not be your first choice in the future. You should always consult with your health care provider when selecting a birth control method.

How do you feel about the methods that were recommended for you?

Do you think this interactive program was a good way to figure out which contraceptives would work best for you?

Want to know more? You can find additional information about topics covered in this chapter at sexuality.jbpub.com.

Chapter 9: Conception, Pregnancy, and Birth

Learning Objectives

By the end of this chapter, you should be able to:

- Explain what happens during the process of conception and implantation.

- Explain what happens developmentally to the mother and embryo and fetus during the three trimesters of pregnancy.

- Describe the concept of prenatal care, and discuss the options for birth attendants and place of birthing.

- Explain the many behaviors that can affect pregnancy outcomes, including use of drugs, diseases, and Rh incompatibility.

- Identify maternal health problems that may be experienced during pregnancy.

- Describe the physical and emotional reactions common during the three stages of giving birth.

- Cite the causes of infertility and describe the various methods of treating it.

Chapter 9

CONCEPTION, PREGNANCY, AND BIRTH

© 2007 Jones and Bartlett Publishers

CHAPTER OBJECTIVES

- Explain what happens during the process of conception and implantation.
- Explain what happens developmentally to the mother and embryo/fetus during the three trimesters of a pregnancy.

© 2007 Jones and Bartlett Publishers

CHAPTER OBJECTIVES

- Describe the concept of prenatal care, and discuss the options for birth attendants and place of birthing.
- Explain the many behaviors that can affect pregnancy outcomes, including drugs, diseases, and Rh incompatibility.

© 2007 Jones and Bartlett Publishers

Notes

_____

_____

_____

_____

_____

_____

_____

_____

_____

_____

_____

_____

_____

_____

_____

_____

_____

_____

_____

_____

_____

_____

_____

_____

_____

_____

_____

_____

_____

_____

_____

_____

_____

CHAPTER OBJECTIVES

- Identify the maternal health problems that may be experienced during pregnancy.
- Describe the physical and emotional reactions common during the three states of giving birth.
- Cite the causes of infertility and describe the various methods of treating it.

IN OTHERS' WORDS...

- "We find a delight in the beauty and happiness of children that makes the heart too big for the body."

—_Ralph Waldo Emerson_

CREATING A NEW LIFE

- Fertilization
- Implantation

Notes

_____
_____
_____
_____
_____
_____
_____
_____
_____
_____
_____
_____
_____
_____
_____
_____
_____
_____
_____
_____
_____
_____
_____
_____
_____
_____
_____
_____
_____
_____
_____
_____
_____
_____
_____
_____
_____
_____

CREATING A NEW LIFE

- Pregnancy
  - After conception a woman is in a state of pregnancy, which lasts for the time it takes the fetus to develop
  - Usually nine calendar months
- Confirming pregnancy
  - Presumptive signs
  - Probable signs
  - Positive signs
  - Pregnancy tests
    - Human chorionic gonadotropin (HCG)

FETAL DEVELOPMENT

- The first trimester
  - Weeks 1–12
  - When third month begins, developing child is called a fetus

7th WEEK

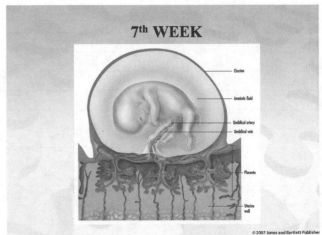

Notes

_____

_____

_____

_____

_____

_____

_____

_____

_____

_____

_____

_____

_____

_____

_____

_____

_____

_____

_____

_____

_____

_____

_____

_____

_____

_____

_____

_____

_____

_____

_____

_____

_____

_____

_____

_____

_____

FETAL DEVELOPMENT

- The second trimester
  - 4–6 months
  - Quickening—movements of fetus felt by mother
  - A baby born at this stage probably would not survive

© Jones and Bartlett Publishers

© 2007 Jones and Bartlett Publishers

FETAL DEVELOPMENT

- The third trimester
  - 7–9 months
  - Presentation—fetal position
  - Preparing for birth

© 2007 Jones and Bartlett Publishers

FETAL DEVELOPMENT

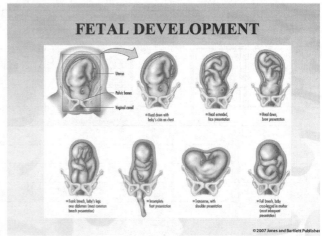

© 2007 Jones and Bartlett Publishers

Notes

PREPARING FOR CHILDBIRTH

- Birth attendant options
  - Obstetrician
  - Midwife
- Birthing alternatives
  - Hospital birth
  - Home birth
  - Freestanding birthing centers

© 2007 Jones and Bartlett Publishers

BEARING A HEALTHY INFANT: PRENATAL CHOICES

- Prenatal care
  - Health care during pregnancy
- Nutrition and weight gain
  - Important to monitor
  - Increased RDAs
  - Vitamin supplements
- Exercise during pregnancy
  - Has many health benefits

© 2007 Jones and Bartlett Publishers

THREATS TO HAVING A HEALTHY INFANT

- Drugs and other substances
  - Any drug can potentially pass through the placenta to the fetus
- Diseases
  - Can pass from mother to fetus
- Rh incompatibility
- Testing for disorders

© 2007 Jones and Bartlett Publishers

MATERNAL HEALTH PROBLEMS DURING PREGNANCY

- Hypertension—blood pressure above normal
- Nausea and vomiting—morning sickness
- Hemorrhoids—varicose veins of the anal area
- Other conditions
  - Chlosama—the mask of pregnancy
  - Stretch marks
  - Hair loss
  - Braxton-Hicks contractions

© 2007 Jones and Bartlett Publishers

CHILDBIRTH

- **Labor & Delivery**

(a) Early first-stage labor
(b) Later first-stage labor: the transition
(c) Early second-stage labor
(d) Third-stage labor: delivery of afterbirth

© 2007 Jones and Bartlett Publishers

CHILDBIRTH

- Delivery of placenta
- Drugs used in childbirth
- Natural childbirth
- Cesarean section
- Premature birth

© 2007 Jones and Bartlett Publishers

BREAST FEEDING

© Kari Weatherly/Photodisc/Getty Images

- Lactation
- Colostrum
- Benefits

© 2007 Jones and Bartlett Publisher

HORMONAL INFLUENCES ON PRENATAL DEVELOPMENT

- Becoming male or female
  - Normal sexual differentiation
  - Abnormal sexual differentiation

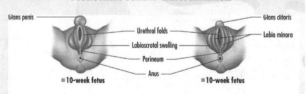

Glans penis — Glans clitoris
Urethral folds — Labia minora
Labioscrotal swelling
Perineum
Anus
■ 10-week fetus   ■ 10-week fetus

© 2007 Jones and Bartlett Publisher

INFERTILITY

- Treatment for infertility
  - Semen analysis
  - Basal body temperature recordings
- Assisted reproductive technologies (ART)
  - Artificial insemination
  - In vitro fertilization (IVF)
  - Gamete intrafallopian transfer (GIFT)

© Photos.com

© 2007 Jones and Bartlett Publisher

IN OTHERS' WORDS...

"To become a father is not hard, to be a father is, however."
—*Wilhelm Busch*

© LiquidLibrary   ©2007 Jones and Bartlett Publisher

BIOLOGICAL FACTORS INFLUENCING PREGNANCY/BIRTH

- Hormones—gender differentiation
- Physiological cycles and changes in fetus
- Physical appearance of mother changes
- Genetic characteristics

©2007 Jones and Bartlett Publisher

SOCIOCULTURAL FACTORS INFLUENCING PREGNANCY/BIRTH

- Socioeconomic status influences infant and maternal health.
- Religion, culture, and ethnic heritage influence beliefs about pregnancy and birth.
- Family, peers, and neighbors provide advice and assistance to new parents.

©2007 Jones and Bartlett Publisher

Notes

_____

_____

_____

_____

_____

_____

_____

_____

_____

_____

_____

_____

_____

_____

_____

_____

_____

_____

_____

_____

_____

_____

_____

_____

_____

_____

_____

_____

_____

_____

_____

_____

_____

_____

_____

PSYCHOLOGICAL FACTORS INFLUENCING PREGNANCY/BIRTH

- Emotions influenced by hormones. Postpartum can be associated with depression.
- Learned attitudes and behaviors often exhibited by pregnant couple.
- Woman's body image changes.

© 2007 Jones and Bartlett Publishers

Chapter 9 Summary: Fill in the Blanks

Creating a New Life

The phases of childbearing are conception, implantation, development, and birth (parturition). A presumptive sign of pregnancy is a missed menstrual period, but pregnancy is normally confirmed by analyzing a blood or urine sample for the presence of the hormone _____ _____ _____ (HCG).

Fetal Development

Pregnancy is divided into three periods called trimesters. The first trimester encompasses the first 12 weeks of pregnancy, the second trimester consists of weeks 13 through 24, and the last trimester includes weeks 25 until delivery.

Throughout the pregnancy the _____ allows nourishment, waste, and antibodies to pass between mother and fetus and protects the fetus from bacteria.

In the first trimester the embryo's physiological systems and body parts begin to form. By the end of the second month, the embryo is about 1¼ inches long. By the 9th week, the developing baby is called a _____. In the second trimester, the greatest amount of fetal growth occurs. The mother can begin to feel fetal movements referred to as _____. In the third trimester, the fetus settles into its birthing position, or _____. By the end of the _____ month, it is generally believed the fetus could survive with the help of a neonatal intensive care unit if it is born prematurely. The fetus' skin is covered with a waxy protective substance called _____.

Bearing a Healthy Infant: Prenatal Choices

Arranging for qualified prenatal care, considering available modes of delivery, maintaining general health and proper nutrition, and understanding the stages of pregnancy, labor, and delivery are all important to maintaining maternal and fetal well-being.

Threats to Having a Healthy Infant

Diseases in the pregnant woman, smoking, drinking, taking drugs (prescribed or otherwise), and genetic disorders all pose risks to the fetus. Maternal serum alpha-fetoprotein (MSAFP) testing, _____ sampling (CVS), and amniocentesis can detect some of the possible birth defects early in a pregnancy.

Maternal Health Problems during Pregnancy

Hypertension, the very serious forms of hypertension known as **preeclampsia** and **eclampsia**, and serious persistent vomiting all pose possible risks to pregnant women.

Childbirth

The beginning of labor is characterized by contractions of the uterus, thinning and _____ of the cervix, and the descent of the fetus (usually head first) into the vagina. When normal delivery would threaten the health of the mother or child, the fetus and placenta may be delivered by cesarean section and incision in the abdomen and uterus.

For some couples natural or prepared childbirth—following the practices of Lamaze, Bradley, or Leboyer—can take the place of conventional hospital deliveries in which the woman is moderately to heavily drugged. These modes make it possible for couples and sometimes other family members to share in the delivery and for some deliveries to take place at home or at a birthing center.

General anesthetics, sometimes used during labor to inhibit pain, not only depress the central nervous system of the mother, they also cross the placental barrier and reach the fetus. Local anesthetics and analgesics, however, reduce the perception of pain and other sensations in the cervix or the whole pelvis without affecting the fetus.

Breastfeeding

The production of breast milk is stimulated after delivery by the pituitary hormone _____. Breastfeeding provides natures perfect formula, ensures the transfer of antibodies from the mother to the newborn, and—for some women—allows for a special physical closeness and emotional bond with the child (though the bond can also be established with a bottle-fed baby).

Sexual Activity During Pregnancy and After Delivery

Intimacy and most forms of sexual activity can be experienced during a normal pregnancy and as soon after delivery as the woman feels comfortable and her physician approves. Ideally, family bonding starts at birth and, whenever possible, both parents should have early physical contact with the newborn.

Hormonal Influence on Prenatal Development

Every egg contains one X chromosome. If a Y chromosome is present in the sperm at conception, testes start to develop;

if a second X chromosome is present then _____ start to develop. Each secrete different hormones which determines the formation of the other sexual organs.

Hermaphroditism is a condition in which organs of both genders are present. True hermaphrodites have both ovarian and testicular tissues. Pseudohermaphrodites have gonads that match their chromosomal makeup, but their other reproductive organs are mixed.

Infertility

Infertility, a problem experienced by large numbers of Americans, is as likely to be caused by a problem in a woman as in a man. Among the causes of infertility are untreated gonorrhea and chlamydia, mumps, sickle-cell disease, several different medications, age, and toxic substances. Diagnosis of infertility may include semen analysis, basal body temperature recordings, an evaluation of ovulatory function, tubal patency test, postcoital examination, hormone monitoring, cervical mucus evaluation, ultrasonography, and hysterectomy.

Infertility can be treated successfully in many ways including artificial insemination, _____ (IVF), gamete intra-fallopian transfer (GIFT), and zygote intrafallopian transfer (ZIFT).

Focus on the Facts

Use the following table to help organize your review of the changes and health care issues occurring during the three trimesters of pregnancy highlighted in this chapter.

Prenatal Care Issues or Tests	Characteristics of Fetus	Physical and Emotional Changes in Mother
First Trimester (Weeks 1–12)		
Second Trimester (Months 4–6)		
Third Trimester (Months 7–9)		

Test Your Knowledge. Are the Following Statements True or False?

Page numbers are provided to help you check your answers as you study.

1. True   False   The fertilized egg is called an embryo until it implants in the uterine wall. (p. 328)

2. True   False   The umbilical cord contains the mother's blood to nourish the fetus. (p. 329)

3. True   False   The pituitary gland produces the hormone *human chorionic gonadotropin (HCG)* when the woman becomes pregnant. (p. 329)

4. True   False   50% of women deliver their babies on their predicted expected date of confinement (EDC). (p. 330)

5. True   False   Ballottement, when a physician feels a floating object in the uterus, is a probable sign of pregnancy. (p. 331)

6. True   False   The average baby is about 20 inches long at birth. (p. 338)

7. True   False   Prenatal care usually begins in the second trimester. (p. 341)

8. True   False   Women should gain 25–35 pounds during a normal pregnancy. (p. 343)

9. True   False   Teratology is a new branch of science searching for reasons for premature birth. (p. 345)

10. True   False   Marijuana and cigarette smoke cannot pass the membrane barrier of the placenta and have no impact on the fetus. (p. 345)

11. True   False   *Diethylstilbestrol (DES)*, a medication to prevent miscarriage, cause problems with fertility and reproductive cancers in the offspring of women who took it. (p. 349)

12. True   False   Lactation usually begins 28–72 hours after a delivery. (p. 362)

13. True   False   Without the Y chromosome, all babies would develop into females. (p. 364)

14. True   False   It is not possible for the genotype, phenotype and internal sexual structures to be different because they are all linked genetically. (p. 364)

15. True   False   Infertility is usually because of a problem with the woman's menstrual cycle. (p. 367)

Match the Following to the Appropriate Pregnancy/Childbirth Concept Described in Your Text

a. Breech delivery

b. Afterbirth

c. Chorionic villi sampling

d. True labor

e. Amniotic fluid

f. Human chorionic gonadotropin

g. Morning sickness

h. Pelvic inflammatory disease

i. Toxemias of pregnancy

j. Parturition

k. Braxton-Hicks contractions

l. Prenatal care

m. Embryonic stage

n. Expected date of confinement

o. Ectopic pregnancy

p. Amniocentesis

q. Chloasma

r. Fetal alcohol syndrome

1. _____ The process of giving birth.

2. _____ The development of the zygote in a location other than the uterus.

3. _____ Weak and slow uterine contractions that occur during the last few months of pregnancy.

4. _____ The delivery of the placenta.

5. _____ A shock absorber, helps maintain a constant temperature in the uterus.

6. _____ A condition of nausea and vomiting common in early pregnancy, thought to be caused by hormonal changes.

7. _____ Due date for normal pregnancy that is usually estimated by Nagele's rule.

8. _____ Regularly spaced contractions of the uterus, thinning and dilation of the cervix, and a descending of the presenting part of the fetus into the vagina.

9. _____ The stage of prenatal development that includes the first 8 weeks of pregnancy.

10. _____ Impaired psychological and physical characteristics common in infants born to alcoholic women.

11. _____ Health care typically consisting of monitoring fetal development, screening for high risk, and education.

12. _____ Technique for prenatal detection of genetic defects involves removal of some chorion and examining the chromosomes.

13. _____ Hypertensive conditions, subdivided into preeclampsia and eclampsia.

14. _____ A yellow to brown patch of skin pigmentation that may appear on the faces of pregnant white women.

15. _____ Infection of the reproductive organs, particularly the uterus, fallopian tubes, and pelvic cavity.

16. _____ Withdrawal of amniotic fluid to determine the presence of fetal abnormalities.

17. _____ The hormone that appears in the blood and urine, providing evidence that a pregnancy has occurred.

18. _____ Infant is born with another part of the body first, rather than head first.

Activity 9.1: Birth Options

What is the difference between the role of an obstetrician and a midwife?

Explain the difference between the following methods of childbirth: (p. 359–361)

Natural childbirth-

Lamaze method-

Bradley method-

Leboyer method-

Cesarean delivery-

Explain the following options used to manage pain in childbirth:

Obstetrical analgesia-

Saddle or epidural block-

Paracervical block-

Activity 9.2: WEB-EX Impact of Infertility

Go to the American Society of Reproductive Medicine web page and click the link for psychology under the patient information heading. Or type in this address: *http://asrm.org/Patients/mainpati.html*

Answer the following questions relating to the psychological impact of infertility.

1. What impact does infertility have on psychological well-being?

2. Who might benefit from psychological counseling when experiencing infertility?

3. How can psychological treatment help individuals/couples cope with infertility?

4. How can I find a mental health professional experienced in working with infertility?

5. What is the RESOLVE group and how can you find out about a RESOLVE group in your area?

Activity 9.3: 3-D Impact of Pregnancy

The text explores the impact of various dimensions of sexuality in pregnancy and birth. However, sometimes it is better to get a personal perspective. Using what you know about the dimensions of sexuality, prepare a list of questions to interview a new mother or a pregnant woman to identify her perspective on how the following dimensions influence her pregnancy:

What is her age? _____   What is her ethnic heritage? _____

Biological Factors:

Psychological Factors:

Sociocultural Factors:

Want to know more? You can find additional information about topics covered in this chapter at sexuality.jbpub.com.

In Focus: Unexpected Pregnancy Outcomes

Learning Objectives

By the end of this chapter, you should be able to:

- Discuss abortion issues, including abortion procedures, legal history, and current attitudes toward abortion.

- Describe the various types of adoptions and the laws surrounding them, including closed and open adoptions, agency adoptions, independent adoptions, and adoptions by relatives.

Unexpected Pregnancy Outcomes Summary: Fill in the Blanks

Abortion

Several alternatives are available to people who experience an unwanted pregnancy. Among these are delivering the baby and parenting the child, abortion, and adoption. Abortion is not a method of contraception and should not be used as such. Spontaneous abortions (_____) are natural terminations of pregnancies. Induced abortions are purposeful terminations of pregnancies.

Eighty-eight percent of all abortions are performed during the first trimester of pregnancy using _____ _____. Medical abortions use drugs such as RU 486 (mifepristone) to induce abortion.

Abortions are usually performed on young, white, unmarried, women who claim no religious affiliation, although minority women have a disproportionate number of abortions. Women seek abortions for three main reasons: having a baby would interfere with their work, education, or other responsibilities; they cannot afford a child; or they do not want to be a single parent or are having problems with their husband or partner. In addition, approximately 13,000 abortions occur because women have become pregnant as a result of having been raped.

Abortions are extremely safe. There is little risk of physical or psychological consequences, and statistically childbirth is ten times more dangerous than is abortion. Most Americans favor the right to abortion, especially if the woman's health is endangered, if the pregnancy is a result of rape, or if the fetus has a serious defect. There is less support for abortion when it is obtained because a baby would interfere with the woman's work or school, when the family could not afford a child, or when the woman is unmarried. Still, approximately half of Americans favor the right to abortion even for these reasons, and _____ % believe the *Roe v. Wade* decision was a good one.

At present our society is wrestling with questions about abortion and human rights—for example, whether abortion is primarily a personal issue to be decided by the woman or couple or a social issue to be decided by the political process. Also under debate is whether the question, when does life begin? is a moral or a scientific one.

The Supreme Court of the United States ruled in 19_____ that (1) during the first three months of pregnancy, abortion is a matter between a woman and her physician; (2) during the second three months, the states can develop regulations that they deem necessary to maintain _____; and (3) after the second three months, the states can prohibit abortions if the mother's health is not jeopardized by the pregnancy. The Supreme Court reaffirmed its decision in 1983 and stated that the government could not interfere with abortion unless justified by "accepted medical practice." This ruling meant that the government could not interfere even in the second trimester and that abortions during this trimester need not be performed in hospitals.

The Court has further decided that the federal government can refuse to pay for or subsidize abortions for women who cannot pay for them themselves (and whose health care is otherwise supported or supplemented by government Medicaid).

Adoption

There are two basic forms of adoption. _____ adoptions are confidential; there is no contact between the birth parents and the adoptive parents. The identity of the birth parents and adoptive parents are kept secret. In open adoptions there is contact between the birth parents and the adoptive parents.

Adoptions can be arranged in three basic ways. In _____ adoptions the parents relinquish their baby to an adoption agency. In _____ adoptions the birth parents select the adoptive parents and relinquish the baby into their care. Adoption by relatives is used when the birth parents want the child to stay in the family.

There is disagreement regarding unsealing adoption records so the birth parents can be identified. Advocates believe adoptees have a right to know their history. Opponents believe that birth parents have a right to privacy. State legislatures are wrestling with this issue in an attempt to be fair to all parties.

Focus on the Facts

Use the following table to help organize your review of the **abortion** and **adoption** research highlighted in this chapter.

Topics	Type of research, findings, or statistics, and notes to help you remember.
Abortion *Procedures* *Laws* *Who?* *Availability* *Emotions* p. 380–398	
Roe v. Wade: *1973* *1983* *1989* *1992* p. 383	
Adoption *Types* *Foster care* *Birth parent* p. 398–402	

Activity IF.2 Unexpected Pregnancy Outcomes WEB-EX

Go to the Adopting.org web site (find it at *www.jbpub.com/sexuality* or at *www.adopting.org/adoptions/learn-about-adoption.html*). Look under "Costs and Fees" for the information below:

Statistics

Domestic public agency adoption: $ _____

Domestic private agency adoption: $ _____

Domestic independent adoption: $ _____

Intercountry private agency or independent adoption: $ _____

Estimates of specific adoption costs

Adoption benefits to help defray adoption costs

Want to know more? You can find additional information about topics covered in this chapter at sexuality.jbpub.com.

Learning Objectives

By the end of this chapter, you should be able to:

- Identify the historical basis for present-day societal, religious, and/or cultural attitudes towards masturbation.

- Cite the prevalence of sexual fantasy, describe its content and function, and note differences in male and female sexual fantasies.

- Describe the role of touch, sight, smell, sound, and taste in sexual foreplay. Then list and describe various positions of sexual intercourse, including their advantages and disadvantages.

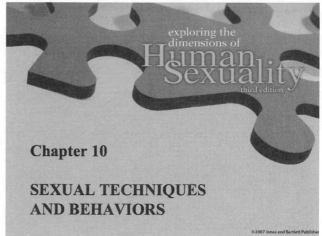

Chapter 10

SEXUAL TECHNIQUES
AND BEHAVIORS

© 2007 Jones and Bartlett Publishers

CHAPTER OBJECTIVES

- Identify the historical basis for present-day societal, religious, and/or cultural attitudes toward masturbation.
- Cite the prevalence of sexual fantasy, describe its content and function, and note differences in male and female fantasies.

© 2007 Jones and Bartlett Publishers

CHAPTER OBJECTIVE

- Describe the role of touch, sight, smell, sound, and taste in sexual foreplay.
- List and describe various positions of sexual intercourse and include their advantages and disadvantages.

© 2007 Jones and Bartlett Publishers

IN OTHERS' WORDS...

- "If sex is such a natural phenomena, how come there are so many books on how to do it?"

  —*Bette Midler*

PSYCHOLOGICAL FACTORS AND SEXUAL BEHAVIOR

- Emotional involvement with a partner plays a role in sexual pleasuring.
- Sexual fantasies are common among males and females.

SOLITARY SEXUAL BEHAVIORS

- Masturbation
- Fantasy

IN OTHERS' WORDS...

"Sex is an emotion in motion."
—*Mae West*

SEXUAL BEHAVIOR WITH OTHERS

- Foreplay
- Senses in sexual behavior

BIOLOGICAL FACTORS AND SEXUAL BEHAVIOR

- Involves five senses
- Physical characteristics can enhance/inhibit sexual activities.
- Foreplay allows for sexual arousal.
- Physical disabilities may limit some sexual activities.
- Safer sexual activities decrease risk of STI/HIV transmission.

IN OTHERS' WORDS...

- "The only unnatural sex act is that which you cannot perform."

  —*Alfred Kinsey*

©2007 Jones and Bartlett Publisher

SEXUAL BEHAVIORS WITH OTHERS

- Oral–genital sexual behavior
  - Cunnilingus
  - Fellatio
  - 69

©2007 Jones and Bartlett Publisher

SEXUAL INTERCOURSE

- Sexual intercourse:
  - Man on top (male superior or "missionary position")
  - Woman on top (female superior)
  - Side by side
  - Rear entry ("dog" position)
- Anal stimulation

©2007 Jones and Bartlett Publisher

SEXUAL BEHAVIOR OF HOMOSEXUALS

- Varied and similar to heterosexual behaviors

- Tribadism—rubbing genitals against someone's body or genital area

©2007 Jones and Bartlett Publisher

SOCIOCULTURAL FACTORS AND SEXUAL BEHAVIOR

- Sexual experience plays a role in what you find arousing.
- Sodomy laws prohibit certain sexual activities.
- Religions may prohibit some sexual activities.
- School sexuality education programs often reflect community standards of acceptable sexual behaviors.

©2007 Jones and Bartlett Publisher

Chapter 10 Summary: Fill in the Blanks

Solitary Sexual Behavior

No physiological harm results from masturbation. Historically, masturbation has been considered a dangerous and negative behavior. Today, the only drawback is the guilt or shame one might ascribe to masturbation. Masturbation is a common sexual behavior with approximately _____% of men and slightly more than _____ of women having at one time masturbated.

Sensuality has many dimensions. Human beings are sexually aroused by fantasies (shared and private), touching, looking, hearing, smelling, tasting, oral-genital activity, and sexual intercourse.

Sexual fantasies are quite prevalent. Kinsey found that _____% of men and _____% of women had sexual fantasies.

Other researchers found sexual fantasies occurred frequently during sexual intercourse and masturbation and usually involved thoughts and images of a loved one, a former lover, intercourse with strangers, oral-genital sex, being found sexually irresistible by others, and having sex forced upon oneself.

Sexual fantasies serve several purposes. They are a source of pleasure, they allow people to test and rehearse various sexual activities, they are helpful in overcoming sexual anxiety, they allow us to be "better" than we really are (at least within the fantasy), and they provide us with a means of fulfilling every desire without hurting ourselves or those we love.

Male sexual fantasies tend to involve more strangers, include more multiple sexual partners, and describe less detail about the setting than do female sexual fantasies. Female sexual fantasies are more likely to describe the partners as having a relationship that involves more than sexual activity, they provide details of the setting, and they portray themselves as less active during the sexual activity.

Sexual Behavior with Others

An important function of foreplay is to allow for vaginal lubrication and erection before penile insertion. Other purposes are to express caring for the person and to enjoy what is sexually pleasing. Common oral-genital activities are cunnilingus, fellatio, and mutual oral-genital stimulation (69). Most positions of sexual intercourse are variations on four basic ones: man on top, woman on top, side-by-side, and rear entry. However, the variations are many, limited only by one's imagination.

Focus on the Facts

Use the following table to help organize your review of the solitary and shared sexual behaviors highlighted in this chapter.

Topics and Researchers	Type of research, findings, or statistics, and notes to help you remember.
Prevalence of Masturbation p. 411	
Prevalence and Content of Sexual Fantasies p. 412	

Topics and Researchers	Type of research, findings or statistics, and notes to help you remember.
Functions of Sexual Fantasy p. 416	
Foreplay Behaviors p. 417	
Cutler et al.; Rensberger; Preti et al. p. 418	
Oral–Genital Behaviors p. 420	

Benefits of Each of the Following Positions for Intercourse
   Man-on-top
   Woman-on-top
   Side-by-side
   Rear entry
p. 422–427	

Sexual Behaviors of Homosexuals p. 427–429	

Test Your Terminology

Fill in the blanks for the terms that fit the following definitions:

1. Self-stimulation of the genitals: _____

2. Thoughts, images, and daydreams of a sexual nature: _____

3. Physical contact preceding sexual intercourse: _____

4. Substances that when secreted have a specific scent found to be sexually arousing: _____

5. Stimulation of the female genitalia by the mouth, lips, and/or tongue of the sexual partner: _____

6. Oral contact with a male's penis: _____

7. Two partners simultaneous stimulation of each other's genitalia orally: _____

8. Licking of the anus: _____

9. Insertion of the penis into the anus: _____

10. Artificial penises: _____

11. Rubbing genitals against someone's body or genital area: _____

Activity 10.1: Sexual Behaviors, a Total Body Experience

Remember Chapter 7, *Human Sexual Response and Arousal*? In that chapter, the brain and five senses were highlighted as essential to sexual functions.

Explain how an individual's thoughts and senses contribute to sexual behaviors highlighted in this chapter:

In what ways might the following influence sexual fantasy?

Your education-

Your gender-

Your family-

Your culture-

Your music choices-

Your age-

Activity 10.2: 3-D Techniques and Behaviors

When it comes to sexual techniques and behaviors, there is a wide range of possibilities. To put it in common terms, it's "different strokes for different folks"! Explain how the following dimensions can influence an individual's choice of techniques and behaviors that they find pleasing.

Biological Dimension:

Psychological Dimension:

Sociocultural Dimension:

Want to know more? You can find additional information about topics covered in this chapter at sexuality. jbpub.com.

Chapter 11: Sexual Orientation

Learning Objectives

By the end of this chapter, you should be able to:

- Define sexual orientation, including heterosexuality, homosexuality, situational homosexuality, and bisexuality. Discuss the validity of the Kinsey continuum.

- Compare and contrast the theories of sexual orientation, including biological, psychological, and socio-cultural theories.

- Discuss homosexual life, including challenges specific to homosexuality.

- Discuss social issues that affect homosexuals.

Notes

Chapter 11

SEXUAL ORIENTATION

© 2007 Jones and Bartlett Publisher

CHAPTER OBJECTIVES

- Define sexual orientation, including heterosexuality, homosexuality, and bisexuality. Discuss the validity of the Kinsey continuum.
- Compare and contrast the theories of sexual orientation.
- Discuss homosexual life, including the challenges specific to homosexuality.
- Discuss social issues that affect homosexuals.

© 2007 Jones and Bartlett Publisher

SEXUAL ORIENTATION

- One's *erotic*, *romantic*, and *affectional* attraction to the same sex, to the opposite sex, or to both
  - Heterosexual
  - Homosexual
  - Bisexual

© 2007 Jones and Bartlett Publisher

_____

_____

_____

_____

_____

_____

_____

_____

_____

_____

_____

_____

_____

_____

_____

_____

_____

_____

_____

_____

_____

_____

_____

_____

_____

_____

_____

_____

_____

_____

_____

_____

KINSEY CONTINUUM

Exclusively heterosexual behavior	0	
Largely heterosexual, but incidental homosexual behavior	1	Heterosexual
Largely heterosexual, but more than incidental homosexual behavior	2	
Equal amounts of heterosexual and homosexual behavior	3	
Largely homosexual, but more than incidental heterosexual behavior	4	
Largely homosexual, but incidental heterosexual behavior	5	Homosexual
Exclusively homosexual behavior	6	

© 2007 Jones and Bartlett Publishers

SEXUAL ORIENTATION

- Bisexuality—attraction to both sexes
  - 9% of women
  - 16% of men
- Asexuality—never felt sexually attracted to anyone
  - 1% of the population
- Homosexuality in the population
  - 2.5%–10% of the population
- Heterosexuality in the population

© 2007 Jones and Bartlett Publishers

IN OTHERS' WORDS...

- "There's this illusion that homosexuals have sex and heterosexuals fall in love. That is completely untrue. Everybody wants to be loved."
  —*Boy George*
- "It seems that the real clue to your sex-orientation lies in your romantic feelings, rather than your sexual feelings. If you are really gay, you are able to fall in love with a man, not just enjoy having sex with him."
  —*Christopher Underwood*

© 2007 Jones and Bartlett Publishers

Notes

THEORIES OF SEXUAL ORIENTATION

- Biological theories
  - Genetic theory
  - Hormonal theory
- Psychological theories
  - Psychoanalytic theory
  - Learned behavior theory

- Integrated theories
- Two landmark studies
  - *LeVay*
  - *Bailey & Pillard*
- Effect of school environment

© 2007 Jones and Bartlett Publishers

HOMOSEXUAL LIFE

- Homophobia
- Coming out
- Gay rights movement
- Legal rights
- Homosexuality and HIV

© 2007 Jones and Bartlett Publishers

BIOLOGICAL FACTORS AND ORIENTATION

- Research into genetic factors for homosexuality has been inconclusive.
- Research into hormonal imbalances has proved inconclusive.

© 2007 Jones and Bartlett Publishers

IN OTHERS' WORDS...

- "If homosexuality is inherited, shouldn't it have died out by now?"

  – *George Booth* (August 1993, *New Yorker* magazine)

© 2007 Jones and Bartlett Publisher

SOCIOCULTURAL FACTORS AND ORIENTATION

- Homosexual students often feel isolated and stigmatized.
- Family life can be disrupted by disclosure of homosexuality.
- Different cultures view homosexuality in different terms.
- Some states have laws making homosexual activities illegal. Gay marriages do not have legal standing.
- Many large corporations have begun to offer employee benefits for domestic partners.

© 2007 Jones and Bartlett Publisher

PSYCHOLOGICAL FACTORS AND ORIENTATION

- Most theories that the influence of mothers or early sexual experiences lead to changes in sexual orientation have been discounted.
- Most homosexuals lead lives as fulfilling and satisfying as those of most heterosexuals.

© 2007 Jones and Bartlett Publisher

Chapter 11 Summary: Fill in the Blanks

Sexual Orientation

A person's sexual orientation is defined as one's erotic, romantic, and affectional attraction to the same gender, to the opposite gender, or both. Sexual identity (orientation) and sexual behavior are two distinct measures, and one is not necessarily consistently predictive of the other.

Homosexuals are attracted to individuals of the _____ gender, heterosexuals are attracted to individuals of the _____ gender, and bisexuals are attracted to _____ genders. Situational homosexuality is sexual behavior limited to specific circumstances in which members of the same gender are generally deprived of contact with the opposite gender.

The Kinsey scale is used to define sexual orientation. The scale classifies sexual orientation along a continuum ranging from exclusively heterosexual behavior all the way through exclusively homosexual behavior, with gradations in between. If someone at one time participated in sexual activity with someone of the same gender, it does not necessarily mean that person is homosexual. Homosexuality is more a function of sexual attraction and desire than of sexual behavior.

The percentage of the population that is homosexual depends on the place on the Kinsey sexual orientation continuum that is used. It also depends on the political interest of those citing the statistics. The percentages cited range from 2% to 10%.

Some bisexuals remain bisexual their whole lives, others are really homosexuals who are in transition and unable to admit to their homosexuality (even to themselves), and others will sooner or later revert to heterosexuality.

Theories of Sexual Orientation

The causes of sexual orientation are unknown. However, several theories have been proposed to explain the development of sexual orientation: biological theories, psychological theories, and learned behavior theories.

Biological theories of the development of sexual orientation include: _____ factors that are inherited and hormonal differences either prenatally or postnatally.

Psychological theories of the development of sexual orientation include: a person fixated at the Oedipal stage of psychosexual development; and family characteristics such as an overprotective and dominant mother and a weak, passive, and detached father.

Learned behavior theories of the development of sexual orientation include: experiencing an unsuccessful and unsatisfying heterosexual relationship, being physically unattractive to the opposite sex, and being recruited to homosexuality through some early childhood experience.

Homosexual Life

Homosexuals are typically happy, well-balanced people just like anyone else. Homosexuality is no longer considered a mental disorder by mental-health experts. _____ is the irrational fear of homosexuality in others, the fear of homosexual feelings within oneself, or the unhappiness with one's own homosexuality.

Homosexuals cannot be easily recognized by their overt behavior or appearance. It is a myth that homosexual men and women really want to be the opposite gender from what they are, that gay men are weak and that lesbians are masculine and strong, and that homosexuals want to seduce children into a life of homosexuality.

Homosexuals often maintain long-standing relationships, although some report many short-term relationships. Homosexuals marry, and their marriages are beginning to be recognized legally.

Making one's homosexuality public is known as "_____." The decision to come out involves several stages: acknowledging one's homosexuality to oneself, accepting one's sexual orientation, and openly expressing one's homosexuality.

The gay rights movement picked up steam in June of 1969 after a raid at the Stonewall—a gay bar in New York City. The raid caused a two-day riot that forever changed the resolve of gays to be treated fairly regardless of their sexual orientation. Presently, homosexuals make up a powerful and influential voting bloc in several major American cities.

Focus on the Facts

Use the following table to help organize your review of the sexual orientation researchers highlighted in this chapter.

Researcher	Type of research, findings, or statistics, and notes to help you remember.
Gay, Lesbian, and Bisexual Adolescents p. 438	
Homosexuality in the Population p. 440–442	
Genetic Theory p. 443–444	
Hormonal Theory p. 444–445	
Psychological Theory p. 445	
Learned Behavior Theory p. 446	

Researcher	Type of research, findings, or statistics, and notes to help you remember.
Effect of School Environments p. 447–451	
Homosexual Life p. 447–451	
Social Issues p. 454–458	
Homophobia p. 459–460	
Legal Rights p. 463–466	

Match the Following Concepts in Sexual Orientation with the Appropriate Definitions

a. Sexual orientation

b. Sexual identity

c. Sexual preference

d. Bisexual

e. Heterosexual

f. Homosexual

g. Gay

h. Lesbian

i. Situational homosexuality

j. Homophobia

k. Heterosexist

l. Come out

1. _____ Accept and make homosexual orientation public.

2. _____ Male or female homosexual.

3. _____ An attitude that reinforces heterosexuality as the privileged and powerful norm.

4. _____ One whose primary erotic, romantic, and affectional attraction is toward members of the other sex.

5. _____ Term formerly used to describe sexual orientation that is now outdated.

6. _____ One whose primary erotic, romantic, and affectional attraction is toward members of one's own sex.

7. _____ One whose erotic, romantic, and affectional attraction is toward both sexes.

8. _____ Homosexual behavior limited to circumstances in which members of the same sex are deprived of contact with the other sex.

9. _____ One's erotic, romantic, and affectional attraction to the same sex, to the opposite sex, or to both.

10. _____ Female homosexual.

11. _____ Inner sense of oneself as a sexual being, including one's identification in terms of gender and sexual orientation.

12. _____ An irrational fear of homosexuality.

Activity 11.1: WEB-EX

At the following web site, you will find links to answer the questions below.
http://psychology.ucdavis.edu/rainbow/html/sexual_prejudice.html
You can also find this site through *www.jbpub.com/sexuality.*

What is sexual prejudice?

What is homophobia?

What is heterosexism?

What do national surveys reveal about the extent of sexual prejudice?

Does personal contact with someone coming out reduce sexual prejudice?

Activity 11.2: Coming Out

Identify the stages in the coming-out process. (p. 460)

Based on the information in this chapter, why do some homosexuals choose to come out and others remain in the closet, keeping their sexual orientation a secret?

Want to know more? You can find additional information about topics covered in this chapter at sexuality.jbpub.com.

Learning Objectives

By the end of this chapter, you should be able to:

- Explain why an infant is a sexual being, including the role that touch plays in development.

- Explain the sexual development of children from preschool through the early elementary years.

- Describe the differences in puberty for boys and girls.

- Identify the three developmental stages of adolescence.

- Compare the findings of various surveys concerning adolescent sexual behaviors and attitudes.

- Discuss the prevalence of sexual abuse and sexual harassment of children and adolescents.

Chapter 12

SEXUALITY IN CHILDHOOD AND ADOLESCENCE

©2007 Jones and Bartlett Publishers

CHAPTER OBJECTIVES

- Explain why an infant is a sexual being, including the role that touch plays in development.
- Explain the sexual development of children from preschool through the early elementary years.

©2007 Jones and Bartlett Publishers

CHAPTER OBJECTIVES

- Describe the differences in puberty for boys and girls.
- Identify the three developmental stages of adolescence.
- Compare the findings of various surveys concerning adolescent sexual behaviors and attitudes.
- Discuss the prevalence of sexual abuse of children.

©2007 Jones and Bartlett Publishers

SEXUAL DEVELOPMENT OF INFANTS AND TODDLERS

- Psychosexual development
- Teaching body parts
- Genital touching
- Gender during the first three years

©2007 Jones and Bartlett Publishers

SEXUAL DEVELOPMENT DURING PRESCHOOL AND EARLY ELEMENTARY YEARS

- Preschool genital touching
- Attraction to parents
- Questions about reproduction
- Preschoolers and sex play
- Elementary school years
- The media as sexuality educator for children

©2007 Jones and Bartlett Publishers

SEXUAL DEVELOPMENT DURING PUBERTY

- Preparing for puberty
- Secondary sex characteristics
  - Pubic hair
  - Breast buds

©2007 Jones and Bartlett Publishers

IN OTHERS' WORDS…

- "The age of puberty is a crisis…. It is the passage from the Unconscious to the Conscious; from the sleep of the Passions to their rages; from careless receiving to cunning providing."

  —*Ralph Waldo Emerson*

© 2007 Jones and Bartlett Publishers

PUBERTY FOR GIRLS

- Breast budding at ages 9–10
- Can begin as early as 7, as late as 13.5 years
- Tanner scale
  - Rates physical sexual development

© Photos.com

© 2007 Jones and Bartlett Publishers

PUBERTY FOR BOYS

- Begins on average during 6th–7th grade. Some begin at 9, others as late as 14 years old.
- Tanner Scale
  - Rates physical sexual development
- Nocturnal emissions
- Gynecomastia

  © Mark E. Stout/ShutterStock, Inc.

  - Increase in glandular tissues around the breasts

© 2007 Jones and Bartlett Publishers

Notes

PUBERTY ISSUES

- Early and late developers
- Imaginary audience
- Emotional changes in preadolescence
  - Conformity with peers
- Masturbation

© 2007 Jones and Bartlett Publishers

IN OTHERS' WORDS…

- "Teenagers are people who express a burning desire to be different by dressing exactly alike."
  —*Anonymous*

- "Adolescence begins when children stop asking questions—because they know all the answers."
  —*Evan Esar*

© 2007 Jones and Bartlett Publishers

SEXUALITY IN ADOLESCENCE

- Adolescent development
- Three stages of adolescence
  - Early adolescence (9–11: girls; 11–15: boys)
  - Middle adolescence (13–16: girls; 14–17: boys)
  - Late adolescence (16: girls; 17: boys)

© 2007 Jones and Bartlett Publishers

DEVELOPMENTAL TASKS

- Physical and sexual maturation
- Independence
- Conceptual identity
- Functional identity
- Cognitive development
- Sexual self-concept

© 2007 Jones and Bartlett Publisher

ADOLESCENT SEXUAL BEHAVIOR

- Sexual orientation
- Sexual behavior is almost universal among American adolescents.

©Barbara Haynor/Index Stock Imagery

© 2007 Jones and Bartlett Publisher

SEXUAL ABUSE OF CHILDREN AND ADOLESCENTS

- Sexual abuse of children
  - Psychological exploitation of children
- Sexual abuse of adolescents
  - Psychological exploitation of adolescents
- Sexual harassment
  - Unwanted sexual behavior

© 2007 Jones and Bartlett Publisher

BIOLOGICAL FACTORS

- Puberty—reproduction becomes possible after menarche and spermenarche.
- Sexual arousal and response are important issues.
- Physical appearance changes dramatically during puberty, affecting body image.
- Growth and development affect self-concept.

© 2007 Jones and Bartlett Publishers

PSYCHOLOGICAL FACTORS

- Emotions dramatically affected by hormones—mood swings
- Body image shaped by puberty
- Sexual experience quicker today
- Self-concept influenced by social status and peers
- Learned attitudes and behaviors tested by physical changes

© 2007 Jones and Bartlett Publishers

SOCIOCULTURAL FACTORS

- Socioeconomic status affects sexual behaviors.
  - Low SES youth have intercourse earlier and have more STIs and births.
- Religion and ethnicity heritage affect beliefs about sexuality and permissiveness.
- Double standard for boys and girls exists in many cultures.
- Media and ad information convey information to teens.
- Friends often convey false information about sexual behaviors to teens.

© 2007 Jones and Bartlett Publishers

Chapter 12 Summary: Fill in the Blanks

Sexual Development in Infants and Toddlers

Biological sexual development begins during _____. Our sexuality undergoes cyclical changes, as well as stages of physical, intellectual, and emotional development. Infants develop sexually through touch—kissing, hugging, holding—which helps to cement the parent–child bond. Touch is one of the first ways a baby learns it is loved and psychosexual development begins.

Parents teach children names for body parts (such as head, shoulders, knees, and toes). When parents fail to teach names for genitals, children may sense shame or guilt about their sexual organs. One way in which infants express their sexuality is by touching their genitals. This exploration is not purposeful and is not directed at orgasm. Gender stereotypes affect the way parents feel about and raise their children.

Sexual Development in Preschool and Early Elementary Years

A child's questions about reproduction should be answered in terms of where—where the baby comes from and where

it was before it was born. Preschoolers are curious about their bodies and may engage in harmless "_____ play." During the early elementary school years, children continue to be interested in sexual issues—the Freudian concept of

_____ is incorrect. During this stage, love maps are developed in our brains, helping to develop an idealized romantic and sexual partner. The media is a prominent sexuality educator for children. Sexual content on TV, in movies, or in print media influences children's views of sexuality.

Sexual Development During Puberty

Puberty is the stage of maturation when a human becomes capable of sexual reproduction. _____ sexual characteristics begin around age 8 for girls and age 9 for boys. It takes from four to five years after the first physical changes to reach full reproductive potential.

Puberty for girls begins with secondary sexual characteristics of _____ development, as well as pubic and underarm hair. The average age of first period, or menarche, is 12½. The onset of menarche may be dependent on the proportion of body fat, with the mean body fat at menarche at 24%. Puberty for boys begins with secondary sexual

characteristics of increased size of _____, and pubic and underarm hair. The age of ability to ejaculate sperm, or spermenarche, is usually about age 13 or 14.

Age of onset of puberty varies widely for both males and females, which brings up the question, "Am I normal?" With some exceptions for precocious puberty or very late development, normal is what your body has provided for you. Worries about normalcy also affect the emotional and social development of adolescents. Rapid physical changes initiate many psychosocial changes. Adolescents need to test parental (and teacher) authority, begin to feel peer pressure, and begin to develop a sense of identity. During puberty, boys and girls begin to masturbate for sexual pleasure.

Sexuality in Adolescence

Becoming a sexually healthy adult is a key developmental task of adolescence. In early adolescence (females aged _____, males aged _____), physical changes require psychological and social adjustments on behalf of the adolescent and his or her family. Conflicts with parents peak and peer norms become increasingly important. Sexual experimentation of some kind is common, but sexual intercourse is usually limited.

Middle adolescence (females aged _____, males aged _____) brings about major transitions to abstract thinking and a feeling of invincibility. Sexuality and sexual expression are of major importance. Middle adolescents focus on themselves, and assume others will focus on them as well.

Late adolescence (females aged 16 and older, males aged 17 and older) sees teenagers moving toward adult roles and responsibilities. Many are able to think _____ and realize the consequences of their actions. Adolescent developmental tasks include physical and sexual maturation, independence, conceptual identity, functional identity, cognitive development, and sexual self-concept. Most U.S. adolescents engage in some form of sexual behavior, from kissing to intercourse.

Many gay and lesbian adults identify adolescence as a period of confusion about their sexual identity. Gay males believe they might be homosexual at an average age of 17; lesbians at age 18. "Coming out" generally does not occur until adulthood.

Sexual Abuse of Children and Adolescents

About 200,000 children are reported to be sexually abused each year, _____% by someone in the family or close to the family. Girls are more likely to be abused than boys, and males are more likely to be assailants than women. Six percent of boys and 15% of girls are sexually assaulted by their 16th birthday. Sexual harassment is a fact of life at most middle and high schools. In fact, 85% of girls and 76% of boys grades 8–11 reported they had been victims.

Focus on the Facts

Use the following table to help organize your review of the sexuality in childhood and adolescence researchers highlighted in this chapter.

Researchers/topics	Characteristics, findings, or statistics, and notes to help you remember.
Infants p. 474–478	
Gender, First 3 Years p. 478–480	
Preschool and Early Elementary Years p. 480–483	
Elementary Years p. 483–484	
Media as Sexuality Educator of Children p. 484	

Researchers/topics	Characteristics, findings, or statistics, and notes to help you remember.
Puberty: Girls p. 485–486	
Puberty: Boys p. 486–487	
Early and Late Developers p. 487	
Emotional Changes in Preadolescence p. 488	
Sexuality in Adolescence p. 489–490	
Three Stages of Adolescence p. 494–496	
Adolescent Developmental Tasks p. 496–497	

Researchers/topics	Characteristics, findings, or statistics, and notes to help you remember.
Sexual Orientation p. 499	
Adolescent Sexual Behavior p. 500–505	
Sexual Abuse of Children p. 505–508	
Sexual Abuse of Adolescents p. 509	
Sexual Harassment p. 509–510	

Test Your Knowledge. Are the Following Statements True or False?

Page numbers are provided to help you check your answers as you study.

1. True False   Infant boys may experience erections. (p. 475)

2. True False   Many parents play with and hold their baby girls differently than baby boys. (p. 479)

3. True False   Many 5- to 8-year-olds are very interested in sexual issues. (p. 483)

4. True False   An internal locus of control is the idea that one's sense of identity is personally defined and not dependent on the scripts of others. (p. 484)

5. True False   Menarche is the first sign of puberty in girls. (p. 485)

6. True False   Breast development in boys is a condition called gynecomastia. (p. 487)

7. True False   Precocious puberty in boys is an indication that something is wrong. (p. 487)

8. True False   A majority of boys begin masturbating between the ages of 13 and 15. (p. 489)

9. True False   Secondary sex characteristics don't appear until middle adolescence. (p. 485)

10. True False   By the age of 18 years, more than ¾ of teenagers have engaged in heavy petting. (p. 500)

11. True False   Seven percent of girls and 4% of boys younger than age 12 report they have been sexually abused. (p. 505)

Match the Following Childhood and Adolescent Concepts with the Appropriate Definitions

a. Sexual harassment

1. _____   Decreased activity of the gonads that may result in retardation of growth and sexual development.

b. Cognitive development

2. _____   Refers to an individual's perception of the main causes of events in life. More simply, is life destiny controlled by self (internal locus) or by forces such as fate or other people (external locus)?

c. Sexual self-concept

3. _____   Ability to see a situation from another person's point of view.

d. Hypogonadism

4. _____   Explains the ability to think concretely or abstractly.

e. Locus of control

5. _____   The typical "teenage years," usually ages 13–16 for females and ages 14–17 for males.

f. Late adolescence

6. _____   First stage defined by pubertal changes—usually ages 9–13 years for females and ages 11–15 years for males.

g. Sexual abuse

7. _____   Unwanted sexual behavior that interferes with the student's life.

h. Conformity with peers

8. _____   What adult roles will I play in the world?

i. Early adolescence

9. _____   Glandular tissue development in the breasts of boys.

j. Precocious puberty

10. _____   Desire to be like everyone else.

k. Gynecomastia

11. _____   Who am I as a sexual being?

l. Social cognition

12. _____   Pubertal development before the age of 7 years.

m. Tanner scale

13. _____   The psychological exploitation or infliction of unwanted sexual contact on one person.

n. Middle adolescence

14. _____   Period of transition to adulthood, beginning usually at age 16 years for females and 17 years for males.

o. Functional identity

15. _____   Scale developed for measuring pubertal development in boys and girls.

p. Psychosexual development

16. _____   A process of developing a close physical and psychological relationship with one's caregiver. (p. 476)

q. Bonding

17. _____   The blending of sexual aspects of one's development with other psychological factors. (p. 476)

Activity 12.1: Puberty & Sexuality in Adolescence

Identify the *secondary sexual characteristics* of males and females which appear during adolescence:

Males   Females

Explain the concept of *imaginary audience* as it relates to adolescent development.

What can adults (parents, teachers, relatives) do to help adolescents develop into sexually healthy adults?

Explain the Following Adolescent Developmental Tasks:

Physical and sexual maturation:

Independence:

Conceptual identity:

Functional identity:

Cognitive development:

Sexual self-concept:

Activity 12.2: 3-D Child and Adolescent Sexuality

Think back to your experiences with puberty and your teen years. Explain how the following factors influence your sexuality today:

Biological Factors and You

Sociocultural Factors and You

Psychological Factors and You

Want to know more? You can find additional information about topics covered in this chapter at sexuality.jbpub.com.

Learning Objectives

By the end of this chapter, you should be able to:

- Discuss the major theories of love and sexuality.

- Describe the typical college relationship, including sexual activities.

- Cite the factors that have led to the increase in the number of single people and the postponement of marriage.

- Evaluate the advantages and disadvantages of cohabitation.

- Describe the characteristics of a happy marriage.

- Discuss the reasons for the high number of divorces.

- Describe the changes that occur during the aging process.

- Discuss the sexuality challenges for the disabled and ill, as well as how to overcome them.

Chapter 13

SEXUALITY IN ADULTHOOD

©2007 Jones and Bartlett Publisher

CHAPTER OBJECTIVES

- Discuss the major theories of love and sexuality.
- Describe the typical college relationship, including sexual activities.
- Cite the factors that have led to the increase in the number of single people and the postponement of marriage.

©2007 Jones and Bartlett Publisher

CHAPTER OBJECTIVES

- Evaluate the advantages and disadvantages of cohabitation.
- Describe the characteristics of a happy marriage.
- Discuss the reasons for the high number of divorces, as well as divorce's effect on the family.

©2007 Jones and Bartlett Publisher

Notes

_____

_____

_____

_____

_____

_____

_____

_____

_____

_____

_____

_____

_____

_____

_____

_____

_____

_____

_____

_____

_____

_____

_____

_____

_____

_____

_____

_____

_____

_____

CHAPTER OBJECTIVES

- Describe the physical, psychological, and sociocultural changes that occur during the aging process.
- Discuss the sexuality challenges for the disabled and ill, as well as how to overcome them.

© 2007 Jones and Bartlett Publishers

LOVE AND SEXUALITY

- Theories of love
  - _Eros, agape, storge, ludus, and mania_
- Types of love
  - _Sternberg's types (phases) of love_
- Characteristics of romantic love
- Love as a relationship develops
- Love problems
- What causes attraction?

© 2007 Jones and Bartlett Publishers

SEXUALITY DURING THE COLLEGE YEARS

- Type of relationship
- Safer sexual activities and college students

© Photos.com   © 2007 Jones and Bartlett Publishers

SINGLEHOOD

- Increasing delay in entering committed relationships
- Singlehood as a temporary situation

© 2007 Jones and Bartlett Publisher

IN OTHERS' WORDS…

- "A woman without a man is like a fish without a bicycle."

  —*Gloria Steinem*

- "A Man without a Wife is but half a Man."

  —*Benjamin Franklin*

© 2007 Jones and Bartlett Publisher

COHABITATION

- Advantages to cohabitation
  - Domestic partner benefits
- Disadvantages
  - Societal pressure/discrimination
- Are cohabitations successful?

© 2007 Jones and Bartlett Publisher

MARRIAGE

- Attraction of marriage
- Choosing a life partner
- Promoting a happy life-long commitment
- Types of marriage
- Sexual behavior in marriage
- Extramarital relationships

© Ingram Publishing/Alamy Images

© 2007 Jones and Bartlett Publishers

IN OTHERS' WORDS…

- "Should I marry or not?"
  "Whichever you do you will repent it."
  —*Socrates*

- "Therefore, a man leaves his father and mother and cleaves to his wife, and they become one flesh."
  —Genesis 2:24

© 2007 Jones and Bartlett Publishers

DIVORCE

- Single-parent families
  - Increased from 6% in 1970 to 28% in 2004
  - Among African Americans, 56% of children under 18 live with a single parent
    - 31% of Hispanic children
    - 14% of Asian children

© AbleStock

© 2007 Jones and Bartlett Publishers

Notes

SEXUALITY AND AGING

- Physiology of aging
  - Psychological changes
  - Social changes
- Barriers to sexual activity in later years
- Aging and safer sexual activities
- Homosexuality among the aging

© 2007 Jones and Bartlett Publishers

SEXUALITY FOR THE PHYSICALLY AND MENTALLY CHALLENGED

- Physical disabilities
- Sexuality and illness
- Sexuality of the mentally challenged
- Personal and social support

© 2007 Jones and Bartlett Publishers

BIOLOGICAL FACTORS

- Physiological changes such as menopause or androgen-receptor sensitivity affect sexuality for the aging.
- Elderly can still have satisfying sexual relationships.
- Illness or physical challenges can affect sexuality.
- Nearly 30 million men suffer from erectile dysfunction.

© 2007 Jones and Bartlett Publishers

PSYCHOLOGICAL FACTORS

- Romantic love characterized by strong feelings of elation, sexual desire, anxiety, and arousal.
- Happy relationships help people handle negative emotions and deal w/conflict.
- Divorces result in emotional scars for partners and children.

© 2007 Jones and Bartlett Publisher

SOCIOCULTURAL FACTORS

- Most Americans attracted to people w/same sociocultural dimensions—race, ethnicity, religion, age, and social class.
- Common societal expectation exists for people to eventually marry.
- People postponing age at first marriage.
- Laws regarding divorce vary.

© 2007 Jones and Bartlett Publisher

Chapter 13 Summary: Fill in the Blanks

Love and Sexuality

Love has been classified in many ways. Greek philosophers described love as passionate, selfless, playful, and consuming. Fromm distinguished brotherly love, motherly love, erotic love, and self-love. Maslow described "Being love" as unselfish love and "Deficiency love" as a selfish type of love. Romantic love consists of companionship, intimacy, caring, commitment, sexual activity, and romance. Most North Americans are attracted to someone who shares the same _____ and attitudes, as well as sociocultural similarities.

Sexuality During the College Years

Studies point to a greater acceptance of sexuality on campus currently than in the 1960s. College students also tend to be serially monogamous. College students do not practice safer sexual activities. Studies show that condom use is relatively rare, partners do not know each other's sexual histories, and many believe they have been lied to regarding sexual activities.

Singlehood

For most heterosexual young adults, singlehood is a temporary status. The great increase in the population of singles is due to _____. Singles delay marriage due to economic constraints, more positive social attitudes toward being single, caution over high divorce rates, and more effective contraceptives. The number of people who never marry has increased since _____.

Cohabitation

Cohabitation refers to people who live together and _____ without being married. Nearly 4.1 million heterosexuals cohabited in 1997, eight times more than in the early 1960s. Societal attitudes toward cohabitation have become much more positive, in part because of the large numbers of cohabitors. However, cohabitors still face discrimination in housing, insurance, taxes, child custody, and other areas. And cohabitors do not enjoy the legal status of married couples. Studies on whether cohabitation improves chances of a happy marriage are mixed.

Marriage

The marriage rate in 2004 was _____ (marriages per 1,000 population). About half of these people will be divorced and will then remarry. Married couples have sexual intercourse more frequently and experience more sexual pleasure today than previously. Marriage can provide companionship, emotional stability, a sexual outlet, and financial security, as well as improve self-esteem and legitimize reproduction. Extramarital activity can be consensual—in which the couple agrees that it is permissible—or nonconsensual. About _____% of females and _____% of males reported in the NORC study that they had engaged in an extramarital sexual relationship.

Divorce

The effects of divorce on a family are great—financially, socially, and emotionally. Children of divorce have a greater chance of dropping out of school, suffering from mental or emotional problems, becoming addicted to alcohol or drugs, and engaging earlier in sexual activity.

Almost 29% of children live with a single parent; among African-Americans, the rate is _____% for children under 18. Single-parent families suffer from financial and emotional pressures. In addition, parental dating causes new stresses on the family as well.

Sexuality and Aging

Sexuality remains an important part of life into old age. Sexuality in older age is multidimensional. Physiological changes, such as onset of _____ for women and androgen-receptor sensitivity for men, are only one aspect of sexuality for the aging. Psychological changes are often caused by changes in mood, caused by biological and lifestyle changes. Social factors include the way that the socialization of the elderly regarding sexuality was different than it is now.

Biologically, as women age, the vaginal lips do not swell as much during sexual excitement, and vaginal lubrication, as well as the length and width of the vagina, decreases. As men age, the _____ become smaller, the scrotal skin becomes thinner and less elastic, and the seminal fluid becomes thinner and less is produced, and sperm becomes less lively.

Sexuality for the Physically and Mentally Challenged

The sexuality of the disabled, ill, and mentally challenged is often neglected, even though they can live sexually satisfying lives. Nearly 40 million Americans have illnesses or disabilities that limit physical activity, including heart conditions, spinal-cord injuries, severe arthritis, and Alzheimer's disease.

Although the biological dimension is prevalent in a physical or mental disability and illness, the psychological and sociocultural dimensions are also important. Body-image and gender-identity issues arise. The partner of the disabled person also suffers. The couple needs to work together to come to terms with their sexuality issues.

Focus on the Facts

Use the following table to help organize your review of the adult sexuality issues and researchers highlighted in this chapter.

Researchers/Topics	Type of issues, findings, or statistics, and notes to help you remember.
Sternberg's Types of Love p. 520	
Hormonal and Chemical Aspects of Love p. 522	
College Years p. 524–528	

Researchers/Topics	Type of issues, findings, or statistics, and notes to help you remember.
Singlehood p. 528–530	
Cohabitation p. 530–533	
Marriage p. 533–542	
Extramarital Relationships p. 542–545	
Divorce; Single- Parent Families p. 545–550	
Sexuality and Aging p. 550–558	
Sexuality and Physically/ Mentally Challenged p. 558–564	

Match the Following Gender Concepts with the Appropriate Definitions

a. Cohabitation

b. Common-law marriage

c. Nuclear family

d. Peer marriage

e. Stepfamily

f. Nonconsensual

g. Consensual

h. Open marriage

i. Swinging

j. Single-parent family

k. Hysterectomy

1. _____ A married couple and their children.

2. _____ For whatever reason, only one parent who is living with a child or children.

3. _____ Surgical removal of the uterus.

4. _____ A family with children that is formed as a result of remarriage.

5. _____ Swapping of mates for sexual activities.

6. _____ A marriage in which partners allow each other to have intimate and emotional relationships with others.

7. _____ Situation in which people who live together and share a sexual relationship are not married.

8. _____ A married person's engaging in sexual intercourse without the consent of the spouse.

9. _____ Relationship in which partners have equal status.

10. _____ The recognition by some states that heterosexual couples who have lived together for a specified period and have represented themselves as married are in fact legally married.

11. _____ Married person's engaging in sexual activity with the knowledge and permission of the spouse.

Theories of Love: Fill in the Blanks for the Following Types of Love to the Appropriate Definitions.

1. _____ Passionate and/or erotic love.

2. _____ Selfless, giving love.

3. _____ Affectionate love, usually the type parents have for their children.

4. _____ Playful love, where partners keep the relationship at a distance by keeping love at a game level.

5. _____ A love consumed by emotional extremes such as misery, possessiveness, and jealousy.

6. _____ Characterized by a dependent relationship between two people.

7. _____ Characterized by care, responsibility, respect, and knowledge of the loved person.

Activity 13.1: 3-D Advantages and Disadvantages of Relationships

After reading this chapter, explain the advantages and disadvantages to each of the following types of relationships from the biological, psychological and sociocultural perspectives.

	Advantages	Disadvantages
Singlehood		
Biological perspective		
Psychological perspective		
Sociocultural perspective		
Cohabitation		
Biological perspective		
Psychological perspective		
Sociocultural perspective		
Marriage		
Biological perspective		
Psychological perspective		
Sociocultural perspective		

	Advantages	Disadvantages
Extramarital Relationship		
Biological perspective		
Psychological perspective		
Sociocultural perspective		
Divorce		
Biological perspective		
Psychological perspective		
Sociocultural perspective		

Notes

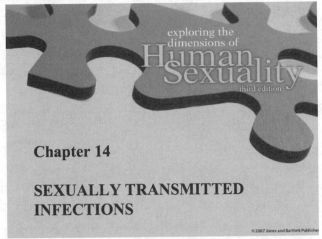

Chapter 14

SEXUALLY TRANSMITTED INFECTIONS

© 2007 Jones and Bartlett Publisher

CHAPTER OBJECTIVES

- Define STIs and SRDs, describe how they are transmitted, and discuss the reasons for their prevalence.
- Discuss the bacterial-based STIs, including incidence, transmission, symptoms and complications, and diagnosis and treatment.

© 2007 Jones and Bartlett Publisher

CHAPTER OBJECTIVES

- Discuss the viral-based STIs, including incidence, transmission, symptoms and complications, and diagnosis and treatment.
- Discuss the ectoparasitic infestations, including transmission, symptoms and complications, and diagnosis and treatment.
- Describe the ways that STIs and SRDs can be prevented.

© 2007 Jones and Bartlett Publisher

IN OTHERS' WORDS...

- "Sex, the invention of a very clever venereal disease."

  —*David Cronenberg*

© 2007 Jones and Bartlett Publishers

WHAT ARE SEXUALLY TRANSMITTED INFECTIONS?

- STI (Sexually transmitted infection) vs. SRD (Sexually related disease)
- Prevalence of sexually transmitted infections

© 2007 Jones and Bartlett Publishers

BACTERIAL INFECTIONS:
CHLAMYDIA

- Symptoms and complications
  - Symptoms mild and often go unnoticed
- Diagnosis and treatment
  - Culture, rapid assay, or fluorescent antibody test
  - Antibiotic treatment

© 2007 Jones and Bartlett Publishers

Notes

_____

_____

_____

_____

_____

_____

_____

_____

_____

_____

_____

_____

_____

_____

_____

_____

_____

_____

_____

_____

_____

_____

_____

_____

_____

_____

_____

_____

_____

_____

_____

_____

_____

BACTERIAL INFECTIONS: *GONORRHEA*

- Incidence
- Transmission
- Symptoms and complications
- Diagnosis and treatment
- Nongonococcal urethritis (NGU)

PELVIC INFLAMMATORY DISEASE (PID)

- Complication of untreated STIs
- Symptoms
- Infertility

Courtesy of the CDC

BACTERIAL INFECTIONS: *SYPHILIS*

- Incidence
- Transmission—spirochete
  - *Treponema pallidum*
- Symptoms and complications
  - Primary
  - Secondary
  - Latent/tertiary
- Diagnosis and treatment

VIRAL INFECTIONS: *HERPES GENITALIS HERPES SIMPLEX VIRUS*

- HSV-1 and HSV-2
  - Four stages of infection
  - Formation of antibodies
  - Development of herpes lesions
- Diagnosis and treatment
  - Most diagnosis made from lesions
  - Culture used to confirm
  - No cure, but effective treatments available

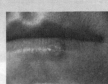

Courtesy of Dr. Herrmann/CDC

© 2007 Jones and Bartlett Publishers

HSV

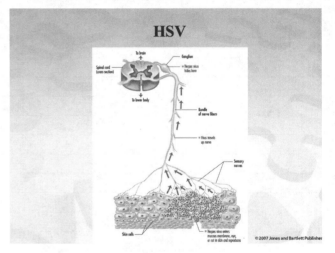

© 2007 Jones and Bartlett Publishers

VIRAL INFECTIONS: *HEPATITIS B*

- Incidence
  - Approximately 80,000 cases in the U.S.
- Symptoms and complications
- Diagnosis and treatment
- Immunization
  - Has been available since 1982

© 2007 Jones and Bartlett Publishers

VIRAL INFECTIONS:
GENITAL WARTS
HUMAN PAPILLOMA VIRUS

- Incidence
- Signs and complications
- Diagnosis and treatment
  - Diagnosed by presence of warts in genital region
  - Treatment but no cure
    - Cryotherapy
    - Polophyllin

© 2007 Jones and Bartlett Publisher

VAGINAL INFECTIONS

- Trichomoniasis
  - A one-celled organism that burrows under the vaginal mucosa

Courtesy of the CDC

- Candidiasis
  - The second most common form of vaginitis (yeast infection)

© 2007 Jones and Bartlett Publisher

ECTOPOPARASITIC INFESTATIONS

- Lice—three kinds:
  - *pediculus corporis*—body louse
  - *pediculus capitus*—head louse
  - *pediculus pubic*—pubic louse (crabs)

Courtesy of W.H.O/CDC

- Scabies
  - Caused by mites; organism lives for up to 2 months

© 2007 Jones and Bartlett Publisher

PREVENTION OF SEXUALLY TRANSMITTED INFECTIONS

- Abstinence
- Monogamy
- Reduce number of sexual partners.
- Refrain from the use of alcohol and other drugs.

©2007 Jones and Bartlett Publisher

PREVENTION OF SEXUALLY TRANSMITTED INFECTIONS

- Discuss STI concerns with potential sexual partners.
- Examine yourself and your partner.
- Use latex condoms.
- Avoid high-risk behaviors.
- Other protective measures

©2007 Jones and Bartlett Publisher

BIOLOGICAL FACTORS AND STIs

- STIs are contracted primarily through sexual contact.
- Individuals with an STI have a higher risk of becoming infected with HIV.
- STIs can be passed to a baby both before and during birth.

©2007 Jones and Bartlett Publisher

PSYCHOLOGICAL FACTORS AND STIs

- STIs can affect individual's feelings about his/her sexuality.
- Infertility caused by undiagnosed STI can have a devastating psychological effect.
- Individuals with genital herpes may worry their symptoms will reappear.

©2007 Jones and Bartlett Publisher

SOCIOCULTURAL FACTORS AND STIs

- Society's unwillingness to confront sexual issues is a major barrier in responding to STIs.
- Some ethnic groups have higher rates of STIs than others. Southern states have higher rates of syphilis than the national average.
- The cost of treating STIs and associated lost productivity is expensive.

©2007 Jones and Bartlett Publisher

Chapter 14 Summary: Fill in the Blanks

What are Sexually Transmitted Infections and Sexually Related Diseases?

Sexually transmitted infections (STIs) are infections that can be contracted through sexual intimacy. There are also diseases of the sexual organs referred to as sexually related diseases (SRDs), which can occur in both sexually active and _____ individuals.

Bacterial Infections

The incidence of gonorrhea has decreased to an all-time low of _____ per 100,000 population in 2003. It is still considered an important communicable disease, however, especially because of the appearance of penicillin- and tetra

cycline-resistant strains. Untreated chlamydia can lead to _____ in men and _____ disease in women. It is often an asymptomatic infection. Women especially should make testing for chlamydial infection a part of their regular checkup.

Syphilis rates have decreased to their lowest level in recent years, thus posing less of a significant public health problem. Syphilis symptoms come and go, but the disappearance of obvious symptoms, without treatment, does not mean that the disease has disappeared.

Viral Infections

Herpes genitalis is of serious concern, because it is recurrent, highly contagious through sexual contact, and as yet has no known cure. Coping with the emotional and psychological problems related to being vulnerable to recurrence and having responsibility to partners is of particular concern to those who have the disease.

Vaginal Infections

Vaginitises are not always sexually transmitted, nor do they imply inadequate hygiene or sexual promiscuity. They may occur from prolonged exposure to moisture (for example, wet bathing suits) or a change in the chemical environment of the vagina. Pubic lice and scabies are _____ that cause irritation and itching.

Ectoparasitic Infestations

There are a variety of ways STIs and sexually related diseases can be avoided. Abstinence, personal commitment, and an awareness of the risks involved in sexual contact—coupled with regular medical supervision, particularly if one suspects exposure—can reduce, if not eliminate, vulnerability.

Focus on the Facts

Use the following table to help organize your review of the sexually transmitted diseases and infections highlighted in this chapter.

Disease/Infection	Incidence	Transmission	Symptoms and Complications	Diagnosis and Treatment
Bacterial				
Gonorrhea p. 578–582				
Nongonococcal Urethritis (NGU) p. 582				
Chlamydia p. 576–578				

Disease/Infection	Incidence	Transmission	Symptoms and Complications	Diagnosis and Treatment
Syphilis 　Primary 　Secondary 　Tertiary p. 582–585				
Viral Infections				
Herpes Genitalis p. 587–592				
Hepatitis B p. 592–593				
Genital Warts p. 585–587				

Disease/Infection	Incidence	Transmission	Symptoms and Complications	Diagnosis and Treatment
Vaginal Infections				
Trichomoniasis p. 593–594				
Candidiasis p. 594–595				
Ectoparasitic Infections				
Pubic lice p. 595–596				
Scabies p. 596–597				

Test Your Knowledge. Are the Following Statements True or False?

Page numbers are provided to help you check your answers as you study:

1. True   False   All states require physicians to report all sexually transmitted infections to state health departments. (p. 574)
2. True   False   Gonorrhea is a viral infection. (p. 578)
3. True   False   HIV is the most common STI in the United States today. (p. 579)
4. True   False   The chancre manifested in primary syphilis is always painful. (p. 584)
5. True   False   Herpes simplex virus can be cured with antibiotic treatment. (p. 587)
6. True   False   There is a vaccine to prevent infection with hepatitis B. (p. 592)
7. True   False   Cryotherapy for genital warts usually ensures the virus will not return. (p. 587)
8. True   False   Trichomoniasis has a curdled vaginal discharge. (p. 593)
9. True   False   Lactobacilli are helpful bacteria that keep the vaginal environment healthy. (p. 595)

10. True   False   When treating an infestation of pubic lice, clothing and bedding must also be cleaned to avoid reinfestation. (p. 596)

11. True   False   If you are monogamous, you are protected from STIs. (p. 598)

Fill in the Correct Term for the Following Definitions:

1. _____ Infections that are primarily contracted through sexual contact.

2. _____ A bacterial STI that commonly starts with inflammation of the mucous membrane lining of the opening of the body.

3. _____ Infection of the reproductive organs, particularly the uterus and fallopian tubes, and the pelvic cavity.

4. _____ The STI caused by the spiral shaped spirochete bacterium *treponem pallidum.*

5. _____ Itching, tingling, or burning sensation occurring where a herpes lesion will appear.

6. _____ A virally caused STI characterized by wart-like lesions on the genitals.

7. _____ The virus that causes genital warts.

8. _____ The type of vaginitis with a foul-smelling, foamy white or yellow-green discharge that irritates the vagina and vulva.

9. _____ Bacteria in the vagina that aid in keeping it healthy.

10. _____ The parasite commonly referred to as crabs.

11. _____ Skin irritation caused by a tiny mite that is transferred from one person to another by close contact, sexual or otherwise.

Activity 14.1: An Ounce of Prevention

Conduct an informal interview of fellow students (but not from this class!) regarding their feelings about the pros and cons of the following STI prevention methods for college students:

	Pros	Cons
Abstinence		
Monogamy		
Reducing the number of sexual partners		
Refrain from the use of alcohol and other drugs		
Discussing STI concerns with potential partners		
Using latex condoms		

Based on the information you gathered from your peers, what do you recommend as an effective strategy for college students to reduce the risk of contracting sexually transmitted infections? Why?

Activity 14.2: WEB EX- What You Don't Know, May Hurt You

Access the Afraidtoask.com web site in the section on the text web site below or at *www.afraidtoask.com/index.html*

Look around at the anatomy and sexually transmitted infection sections of this site to see more pictures and details about common infections that can be sexually transmitted.

Do you think viewing the pictures and information on this site and in your text is motivation to practice some of the prevention methods discussed in your text?

After reading about sexuality education and STIs in your text, do you think this web based format was a good way to learn about STIs and your sexual anatomy?

Activity 14.3: 3-D Sexually Transmitted Infection

Explore the dimensions of sexuality as they relate to sexually transmitted infection.

While sexually transmitted infections are firmly in the "physical" domain, what are the implications for the sociocultural and psychological domains?

Biological Factors:

Psychological Factors:

Sociocultural Factors:

Want to know more? You can find additional information about topics covered in this chapter at sexuality.jbpub.com.

Learning Objectives

By the end of this chapter, you should be able to:

- Describe Acquired Immune Deficiency Syndrome (AIDS), the opportunistic diseases associated with it, and how the HIV virus invades the body and causes AIDS.

- Discuss different treatments for HIV/AIDS, including how the mortality rate has declined as a result of these treatments.

- Cite ways in which HIV infection can be prevented.

HIV and AIDS Summary: Fill in the Blanks

Acquired Immune Deficiency Syndrome

Acquired Immune Deficiency Syndrome (AIDS) is caused by the _____ virus (HIV), which attacks and slowly destroys the body's immune system. The weakened immune system allows other opportunistic conditions to develop, including Pneumocystis carinii and Kaposi's sarcoma (a form of cancer).

HIV belongs to a class of viruses known as _____. HIV attaches to T4 lymphocytes, white blood cells that play an important role in the immune response. Once attached to a T4 cell, HIV enters it and releases its RNA. The RNA is then converted into DNA and combines with the cell's DNA, causing the cell to reproduce HIV.

HIV infection is prevalent throughout the world, with approximately _____ million cases reported in 2004. Sub-Sahara Africa is the world's HIV "hot spot," with South and Southeast Asia second. Whereas HIV is most often transmitted through homosexual contact in the United States, it is usually transmitted through heterosexual contact elsewhere in the world. HIV is the _____ leading cause of death in the United States, but it is the fourth leading cause of death among African-Americans and the fifth leading cause of death among Hispanics.

HIV is found predominantly in semen and blood, but it can also be found in vaginal secretions. Unprotected sex with an infected individual is the most common way that HIV is transmitted, but it is also transmitted through the sharing of needles. HIV testing is initially performed using the ELISA test to determine if HIV antibodies exist in the body. If the ELISA is seropositive, then the _____ _____ test is used to confirm the presence of HIV antibodies. The polymerase chain reaction (PCR) is a test for the presence of HIV (rather than antibodies), but it is costly and, therefore, not routinely employed. Newer tests are available that can be administered in the home or taken orally.

Treatment for HIV and AIDS

Treatment for HIV/AIDS include several drugs. Zidovudine (AZT) is one of the drugs that has been used over the longest period of time. More recently, a triple-drug therapy has been found to be more successful is treating HIV/AIDS. These drugs include nucleoside reverse transcriptase inhibitors, protease inhibitors, and non-nucleoside reverse transcriptase inhibitors.

Preventing HIV Infection and AIDS

The most effective way to prevent HIV infection is to prevent the initiation of high-risk behaviors. Abstinence from sexual intercourse is the most effective. Still, this option is not viable for many people. The next best means of prevention is to make high-risk behaviors less risky. For example, using a _____ during intercourse will lessen the risk of HIV transmission. Refraining from anal intercourse, especially without the use of a condom, will do the same. Of course, engaging in sexual activities with a partner known to be HIV-free will eliminate the chance of transmission.

Focus on the Facts

Use the following table to help organize your review of the HIV and AIDS research highlighted in this chapter.

Topics	Type of research, findings, or statistics, and notes to help you remember.
Incidence of HIV and AIDS p. 611–612	
Transmission p. 613–614	
Stages of HIV Infection p. 615	
Testing for HIV p. 615–617	
Treatment of HIV and AIDS p. 617–619	
Prevention of HIV/AIDS p. 619–622	

Match the Following Definitions to the Appropriate HIV and AIDS Concepts

a. Retroviruses

b. Human immuno-deficiency virus

c. Opportunistic diseases

d. Seropositive

e. Zidovudine

f. Antibodies

1. _____ Diseases that occur in the presence of a suppressed immune system.

2. _____ The result of a blood test for antibodies to HIV that indicate the antibodies have been found in the blood.

3. _____ A group of viruses that, once they invade a living cell, take over the cell and reproduce themselves.

4. _____ A class of proteins secreted by the immune system to fight off disease causing organisms.

5. _____ Antiviral drug (AZT) that slows the replication of the AIDS virus and the course of the syndrome.

6. _____ The virus that causes AIDS.

Activity IF.1 HIV and AIDS: 3-D Impact of HIV/AIDS

After reading this In Focus chapter, summarize the impact of HIV/AIDS on the following dimensions of human sexuality.

Biological Dimension and HIV/AIDS

Psychological Dimension and HIV/AIDS

Sociocultural Dimension and HIV/AIDS

Activity IF.2 HIV and AIDS WEB-EX

Go to The Body web site. (Find it at *sexuality.jbpub.com* or at the web site below.) Under the section on AIDS Basics and Prevention, click on the link to take The Body's unique interactive survey: assess your risk for HIV and other STIs! (Or type in: *www.thebody.com/surveys/sexsurvey.html*)

Take the survey, answering the questions as honestly as you can to assess your risk for HIV infection. Complete the following questions related to the feedback and results of your completed survey.

Do you think people are more likely to answer questions honestly in a web based survey such as this one?

Were you surprised by any of the feedback you received after completing the survey?

Do you think this survey gives an accurate assessment of your risk?

How likely are you to follow the suggestions made in the feedback?

Want to know more? You can find additional information about topics covered in this chapter at sexuality.jbpub.com.

Chapter 15: Sexual Dysfunction and Therapy

Learning Objectives

By the end of this chapter, you should be able to:

- Describe the major male and female sexual dysfunctions, including the desire dysfunctions. Evaluate what makes the inability to perform sexually a clinical dysfunction.

- Identify the multidimensional causes of sexual dysfunction, including the physical, psychological, and sociocultural dimensions.

- Compare and contrast the varied approaches to treating sexual dysfunctions. Explain why so many different models of therapy exist.

Notes

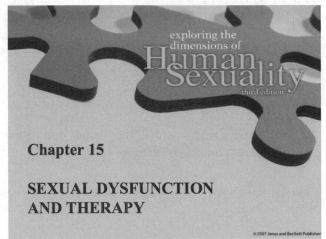

Chapter 15

**SEXUAL DYSFUNCTION
AND THERAPY**

© 2007 Jones and Bartlett Publishers

IN OTHERS' WORDS...

• "When sex is good, it's 10% of a
  relationship. When it's bad, it's 90%."

  —*Charles Muir*

© 2007 Jones and Bartlett Publishers

CHAPTER OBJECTIVES

• Describe the major male and female sexual
  dysfunctions, including the desire dysfunctions.
  Evaluate what makes the inability to perform
  sexually a clinical dysfunction.

• Identify the multidimensional causes of sexual
  dysfunction, including the psychological and
  sociocultural dimensions.

• Compare and contrast the varied approaches to
  treating sexual dysfunctions. Explain why so many
  different models of therapy exist.

© 2007 Jones and Bartlett Publishers

SEXUAL DYSFUNCTION

- Chronic inability to respond sexually in a way that one finds satisfying
  - The amount of sexual dysfunction prevalent in society is difficult if not impossible to determine.
  - Underlying cause may be *either* physical or psychological.

© 2007 Jones and Bartlett Publishers

MALE SEXUAL DYSFUNCTIONS

- Erectile dysfunction
  - Primary erectile dysfunction
  - Secondary erectile dysfunction
- Premature ejaculation
- Ejaculatory incompetence
- Dyspareunia

© AbleStock

© 2007 Jones and Bartlett Publishers

FEMALE SEXUAL DYSFUNCTIONS

- Sexual unresponsiveness
- Orgasmic dysfunction
- Vaginismus
- Dyspareunia

© 2007 Jones and Bartlett Publishers

SEXUAL DESIRE DYSFUNCTIONS

- Inhibited sexual desire
  - *Primary*
  - *Secondary*
- Dissatisfaction with sexual activity frequency
- Sexual aversion—an irrational fear of sexual activity

SEXUAL DYSFUNCTION AND SELF-ESTEEM

- Sexual functioning is closely connected to self-esteem.

- Fear that partners will seek other sexual partners

CAUSES OF SEXUAL DYSFUNCTION

- Physical causes
- Psychological causes
- Cultural causes
- Sexual dysfunction and aging
  - Sex remains an important and vital part of life
  - "Everything we do may be slower, but we have more time."

TREATING SEXUAL DYSFUNCTION: APPROACHES TO SEXUAL THERAPY

- PLISSIT model—permission, limited information, specific suggestion, and intensive therapy
- Masters and Johnson model
- Kaplan's model
- Other approaches to sexual therapy

©2007 Jones and Bartlett Publishers

TREATING ERECTILE DYSFUNCTION

- Injection therapy
- Oral medication
- Bypass surgery
- Venous ligation
- Penile prostheses/implants

©2007 Jones and Bartlett Publishers

TREATING PREMATURE EJACULATION

- Squeeze technique
- Semans's stop-start method

©2007 Jones and Bartlett Publishers

TREATING SEXUAL DYSFUNCTION

- Sensate focus
  - Procedures designed to increase and encourage erotic feelings
- Barbach's technique
  - Used to treat sexual unresponsiveness and orgasmic dysfunction

©2007 Jones and Bartlett Publishers

BEHAVIOR THERAPY MODEL

- Systematic desensitization
  - Overcoming anxiety: the anxiety-provoking stimulus in small steps
- Shaping
  - Rewarding small behaviors along the way to developing the behavior that is the goal of the therapy

©2007 Jones and Bartlett Publishers

CHOOSING A SEXUAL THERAPIST

- Does the person have a degree in a recognized profession related to counseling and therapy?
- Does the person hold a license or certification?
- Is the person certified by AASECT?
- Do you know anyone who has been helped by this therapist?

©2007 Jones and Bartlett Publishers

Notes

BIOLOGICAL FACTORS AND SEXUAL DYSFUNCTION

- Some dysfunctions have a physiological cause.
- Age is sometimes a factor.
- Alcohol, drug abuse, and certain medications or health conditions can interfere with sexual response.

© 2007 Jones and Bartlett Publisher

PSYCHOLOGICAL FACTORS AND SEXUAL DYSFUNCTION

- Sexual functioning is closely connected to self-esteem.
- Gays seeking treatment for disorders must also confront society's negative attitudes about homosexuality.
- Failure to perform as expected can be devastating psychologically and can lead to isolation from further activities for fear of failing.

© 2007 Jones and Bartlett Publisher

SOCIOCULTURAL FACTORS AND SEXUAL DYSFUNCTION

- Sexual double standards may set men and women up for failure.
- Mass media create unrealistic expectations of sexual activity.
- Relationship problems can lead to some disorders.
- Rigid religious convictions may contribute to negative attitudes toward sexuality.

© 2007 Jones and Bartlett Publisher

Chapter 15 Summary: Fill in the Blanks

Sexual Dysfunction

An individual's sexual desire is not constant; it varies according to situational, emotional, and physical factors. Such variation is not dysfunctional. Sexual dysfunction is a _____ _____. Although it is impossible to accurately determine the number of people who have a sexual dysfunction, experts believe that half of all married couples experience sexual difficulties.

Primary sexual dysfunctions are those in which the person has never been functional in a particular sexual activity. Secondary sexual dysfunctions are those in which the person was functional at one time but no longer is. The underlying cause of any sexual dysfunction may be either physical or psychological, but most experts agree that _____ causes, broadly defined, are much more prevalent, causing anywhere from 40% to 90% of sexual dysfunctions.

Male sexual dysfunctions include erectile dysfunction (termed impotence by the lay public), premature ejaculation, ejaculatory incompetence, and _____ (painful intercourse). These sexual difficulties can lead to secondary disorders and to questions of self-worth.

_____ is the inability to achieve and maintain an erection when sexually stimulated. In about 80% of the cases it is the result of organic problems such as diabetes, infections, the use of certain medications, alcoholism, spinal cord injury, or any condition interfering with the flow of blood to the erectile tissue of the penis. The nonorganic causes include guilt, shame, and fear about sexual activity.

_____ is the condition in which the man cannot maintain penile insertion long enough— long enough as judged by the man and his partner—without ejaculating. However, even the experts disagree as to whether a particular situation should be classified as premature ejaculation.

Ejaculatory incompetence means not being able to ejaculate in the vagina. Sometimes, though rarely, this condition can be limited to one partner or to one specific situation. Partial ejaculatory incompetence is when only a "half" orgasm results.

Dyspareunia is _____ and can affect both men and women. Men may feel pain in the penis, testes, or other internal organ; women may feel pain in the vagina or elsewhere in the pelvis. It is possible for dyspareunia to lead to a secondary sexual dysfunction since the fear of pain can interfere with normal sexual responses. Painful intercourse can be caused by infection, insufficient lubrication, allergic reactions to spermicidal creams or foam, or irritation produced from accumulated smegma.

Female sexual dysfunctions include sexual unresponsiveness, orgasmic dysfunction, vaginismus, and dyspareunia. These may result from psychological factors—anxiety, fear, shame, guilt—or from organic factors such as infection or organ trauma.

Sexual unresponsiveness, also called female _____ disorder and known by the lay public as frigidity, is a condition in which the woman experiences little or no erotic pleasure from sexual stimulation. It is manifested physiologically by a lack of vaginal lubrication, lack of vasocongestion, and lack of change in the size of the vagina.

_____ dysfunction is a condition in which a woman does not have an orgasm when sexually stimulated or can achieve an orgasm only during certain situations, with certain sexual partners, or during certain sexual activities. Approximately 10% of women are coitally anorgasmic, and only 30% to 44% of women report they usually experience orgasm during sexual intercourse without having the clitoris simultaneously stimulated. Some sexual therapists argue that if the couple is satisfied with their sexual life and if a woman is orgasmic only during specific sexual activities—for example, only during oral–genital sexual activity—this does not constitute reason for treatment. Only about 5% of orgasmic dysfunction is a result of organic factors.

_____ is the involuntary contraction of the muscles in the outer third of the vagina so as to prevent penetration. In some cases coitus is possible but very painful. Sometimes vaginismus is caused by another sexual disorder; for example dyspareunia. It may also be the result of strong religious teachings against sexual activity, homosexual feelings, or a history of sexual assault.

Sexual desire dysfunctions can include inhibited sexual desire, dissatisfaction with the sexual activity frequency, and sexual aversion. Inhibited sexual desire is a lack of sexual appetite and may be caused if one's sexual partner is unappealing (smelly or dirty) or by pituitary tumors, poor self-esteem, a bad relationship, embarrassment regarding one's body, or a history of sexual abuse. _____ is an irrational fear of sexual activity and is usually caused by severe negative attitudes about sexuality expressed by parents or a history of sexual trauma such as rape or incest, or gender-identity confusion.

Causes of Sexual Dysfunction

Sexual dysfunctions can have physical, psychological, and/or social causes. Physical causes include disease and drug use. Psychological causes include traumatic experiences, abuse, depression, and low self-esteem. It is a myth that older people are not interested in or do not participate in sexual activity.

Treating Sexual Dysfunction

Generally, sexual therapy for both men and women entails three components: (1) an initial period of abstinence from coitus to reduce anxiety and facilitate communication, (2) the use of systematic tactile stimulation and exploration to focus on the giving and receiving of pleasure, and (3) specific technical suggestions and directions that facilitate and reinforce success.

The PLISSIT model of sexual therapy is a stepwise approach to treating sexual dysfunction that begins with permission, moves to providing limited information, then to specific suggestions, and lastly, if needed, to intensive therapy.

Masters and Johnson, Kaplan, behaviorists (such as LoPiccolo), Barbach, Ellis, and McCarthy are only a few of the better known sexual therapists who have proposed models of sexual therapy. Each of these models differs somewhat. Some require a cotherapy team consisting of a man and a woman; others require intensive, long-term therapy; and still others consider irrational beliefs.

Erectile dysfunction can be treated with counseling if caused by psychogenic factors. If caused by organic factors, it can be treated by medication, bypass surgery, venous ligation, penile implants, or inflatable implants.

Premature ejaculation can be treated with the _____ technique developed by Masters and Johnson or the stop-start technique developed by James Semans. Other methods of prolonging ejaculation are the use of condoms, drinking alcoholic beverages, having "small" orgasms, waiting for sufficient vaginal lubrication, switching positions often to decrease muscle tension, and the use of creams designed to decrease sensitivity of the glans penis.

Many specific techniques are available to the sexual therapist. Some of the more common ones are the squeeze technique, the stop-start technique, sensate focus, Barbach's technique, and shaping. Various factors must be considered by a person choosing a therapist: Does he or she have a degree? Is he or she licensed or certified? Does he or she belong to the AASECT? Do you have a referral from someone you trust?

Focus on the Facts

Use the following table to help organize your review of sexual dysfunctions and the current treatment methods highlighted in this chapter.

Topics and Researchers	Type of research, findings, or statistics, and notes to help you remember.
Sexual Dysfunction Characteristics and Incidence p. 632	
Male Sexual Dysfunction p. 635–640	
Female Sexual Dysfunction p. 640–644	
Sexual Desire Disorders p. 644–647	

Topics and Researchers	Type of research, findings, or statistics, and notes to help you remember.
Physical Causes p. 647	
Psychological Causes p. 647–648	
Cultural Causes p. 648–650	
Treating Sexual Dysfunction p. 651–660	

Test Your Terminology

Fill in the blanks for the terms that fit the following definitions:

1. A specific, chronic disorder involving sexual performance. _____

2. Difficulty in achieving and maintaining an erection. _____

3. The inability of a man to maintain an erection long enough to have sexual intercourse. _____

4. The inability of a man to control ejaculation for a sufficient length of time during coitus. _____
   _____

5. A condition in which penile erection occurs during sexual intercourse, but ejaculation does not. _____
   _____

6. Pain in the genital area during sexual intercourse. _____

7. Female sexual arousal disorder where a woman experiences little or no erotic pleasure through sexual stimulation. _____

8. The consistent or frequent inability of a woman to achieve an orgasm. _____

9. The involuntary contraction of the muscles surrounding the vaginal entrance so that the entry of the penis is prevented. _____

10. Lack of interest in sexual activity of various sorts. _____

11. An irrational fear of sexual activity. _____

Activity 15.3: Choosing a Sex Therapist

What is the professional organization that certifies professional sex therapists?

What characteristics should an individual consider or look for in choosing a sex therapist to treat a sexual dysfunction?

Look in your local phone book or on the internet for a certified sex therapist in your area. Who is it and what is his or her address/contact information?

Want to know more? You can find additional information about topics covered in this chapter at sexuality.jbpub.com.

Learning Objectives

By the end of this chapter, you should be able to:

- Discuss how some atypical sexual behaviors exist on a continuum of sexual activity.

- Describe the most common paraphilias.

- Name and define paraphilias other than the most common ones.

- Explain what can be done to treat paraphilias.

- Summarize what is known about sexual addiction.

Atypical Sexual Behavior Summary

Common Versus Atypical Sexual Behavior

Sexual behavior can be considered to occur in gradations or degrees along a continuum. Because many behaviors vary by degrees, it's normal to recognize some degree of atypical behaviors in ourselves—perhaps only in private fantasies.

Unusual or problematic sexual behaviors are scientifically known as paraphilias. There are about 30 different paraphilias, and each exists in fantasy and in reality.

The Most Common Paraphilias

The most common paraphilias include exhibitionism, voyeurism (scopophilia), obscene communication, masochism, sadism, transvestism, fetishism, and partialism. Other paraphilias include bestiality (zoophilia), frottage, necrophilia, troilism, asphyxiophilia, klismaphilia, coprophilia, and urophilia.

Treatment for Paraphilias

Although treatment for paraphilias can be controversial, it includes psychotherapy, behavior therapy, and pharmacological approaches.

Sexual Addiction

Compulsive sexual behavior is sometimes referred to as "sexual addiction." There are practical indicators of compulsive sexual behavior, but there is no agreement about how to best deal with it.

Focus on the Facts

Use the following table to help organize your review of the body image research highlighted in this chapter.

Topics	Type of research, findings, or statistics, and notes to help you remember.
Exhibitionism p. 669	
Voyeurism p. 670	
Obscene Communication p. 671	
Masochism and Sadism p. 671–674	
Transvestism p. 674	
Fetishism p. 675	
Other Paraphilias p. 675–678	
Treatments for Paraphilia p. 678–680	
Sex Addiction p. 680–682	

Match the Following Treatments for Paraphilias with Their Appropriate Descriptions

a. Orgasmic reconditioning

b. Social training

c. Aversion therapy

d. Behavior therapy

e. Antiandrogen drugs

1. _____ Applying learning principles to help people change behavior.

2. _____ Pairing an undesirable sexual behavior to a painful response.

3. _____ Improving a person's social skills.

4. _____ Increasing sexual arousal to socially appropriate stimuli.

5. _____ Chemicals that reduce the sex drive by lowering the testosterone level in the bloodstream.

Activity IF.1 Atypical Sexual Behaviors

Many people feel that what others do in private with their sexuality is their own business. However, some of the atypical sexual behaviors described in this text may impinge on your personal rights without you even realizing it! Fill in the characteristics of the following paraphilias. Explain whether you believe there is a victim or if individuals with these desires should just be allowed to "do their own thing."

Paraphilia	Brief description	Victim or victimless? Why?
1. Transvestite		
2. Asphyxiophilia		
3. Exhibitionism		
4. Klismaphilia		
5. Coprophilia		
6. Partialism		
7. Bestiality		
8. Voyeurism		
9. Troilism		
10. Fetishism		
11. Masochism		
12. Sadism		
13. Frottage		
14. Urophilia		

Want to know more? You can find additional information about topics covered in this chapter at sexuality.jbpub.com.

Learning Objectives

By the end of this chapter, you should be able to:

- Differentiate among rape, statutory rape, stranger rape, and date (acquaintance) rape. Discuss what makes someone rape. Discuss the myths surrounding rape.

- Discuss pedophilia, including the profile of the pedophiliac, incidence and effects of pedophilia, and prevention.

- Describe the incidence of incest and the typical effects on incest victims.

- Summarize important information about violence within marriage, including marital rape and domestic abuse.

- Discuss sexual harassment in the workplace, in schools, on campus, and in the military, and indicate what can be done to prevent and deal with it.

Chapter 16

FORCIBLE SEXUAL BEHAVIORS

© 2007 Jones and Bartlett Publisher

CHAPTER OBJECTIVES

- Differentiate among rape, statutory rape, stranger rape, and date (acquaintance) rape. Discuss what makes someone rape. Discuss the myths surrounding rape.

- Discuss pedophilia, including the profile of the pedophiliac, incidence and effects of pedophilia, and prevention.

© 2007 Jones and Bartlett Publisher

CHAPTER OBJECTIVES

- Describe the incidences of incest and the typical effects of incest victims.

- Summarize important information about violence within marriage, including marital rape and domestic abuse.

- Discuss sexual harassment in the workplace, in schools, on campus, and in the military, and indicate what can be done to prevent and deal with it.

© 2007 Jones and Bartlett Publisher

_____
_____
_____
_____
_____
_____
_____
_____
_____
_____
_____
_____
_____
_____
_____
_____
_____
_____
_____
_____
_____
_____
_____
_____
_____
_____
_____
_____
_____
_____
_____
_____
_____
_____

IN OTHERS' WORDS...

"Men are taught to apologize for their weakness, women for their strengths."

—*Lois Wyse*

© 2007 Jones and Bartlett Publisher

RAPE

- Rape myths
  - Women lead men on
  - Women deserve to be raped
  - Women make false accusations of rape
  - No woman can be raped against her will
  - Most rapists are strangers
- Society and rape
- The rapist

© 2007 Jones and Bartlett Publisher

DATE/ACQUAINTANCE RAPE

- Nonconsensual sex between dating partners
- Risk factors
- Communication
- Ways to help prevent acquaintance rape
  - Challenge myths and stereotypes
  - Talk with friends and give one another the opportunity to be assertive, respectful, honest, and caring
  - Communicate effectively about sexual issues

© 2007 Jones and Bartlett Publisher

DATE RAPE DRUGS

- Rohypnol
- GHB
- Ketamine hydrochloride

© Liquid Library © SuperStock/Alamy Images
©2007 Jones and Bartlett Publisher

INCIDENCE OF SEXUAL ASSAULT

- Statistics are unreliable.
  - However, they can still give us a general picture of what is happening.
    - 1 in 6 women and 1 in 33 men in the U.S. have been victims of rape or attempted rape.
    - 80% of them knew their perpetrators.

©2007 Jones and Bartlett Publisher

CONSEQUENCES OF RAPE

- Rape trauma syndrome
- Fear of intimacy
- Lower self-esteem

©2007 Jones and Bartlett Publisher

RAPE OF MALES

- Male rape in prison
- Male rape by other males
- Male rape by females

© 2007 Jones and Bartlett Publisher

SOCIAL RESPONSES TO RAPE

- Sexual assault crisis centers
- Workshops
- Shelters
- Greater recognition of the need for services and prevention
- Changes in law enforcement personnel
  - Training to become more sensitive
  - More female officers
  - Better cooperation with medical and support personnel
  - Guidelines for handling survivors of sexual assault

© 2007 Jones and Bartlett Publisher

PEDOPHILIA

- The pedophiliac
  - Usually a victim of sexual abuse
  - Typically a male, though female incidence may be higher than reported
- Incidence of pedophilia
  - Often statistics do not differentiate pedophilia from child sexual abuse
  - 44% of rape victims are under 18

© 2007 Jones and Bartlett Publisher

EFFECTS OF PEDOPHILIA

- Childhood
  - Sleeping or eating disturbances
  - Anger, withdrawal, guilt
- Adolescence
  - Shame, poor body image, self-destructive behavior
- Prevention
  - Developing children's competence
  - Helping children recognize abusive situations and disclose victimization

© 2007 Jones and Bartlett Publisher

INCEST

- Sexual behavior between relatives who are too closely related to be married
- Incidence
  - 95% of offenders are male
- Impact
- Intervention
  - Stop sexual abuse and establish a safe environment in the family

© 2007 Jones and Bartlett Publisher

RELATIONSHIP ABUSE

- Marital rape
  - As recently as 1976 no husband could be charged with raping his wife
  - Today it is a crime in all 50 states
- Domestic violence
  - 1/3 of American women

© Photos.com

© 2007 Jones and Bartlett Publisher

Notes

_____
_____
_____
_____
_____
_____
_____
_____
_____
_____
_____
_____
_____
_____
_____
_____
_____
_____
_____
_____
_____
_____
_____
_____
_____
_____
_____
_____
_____
_____
_____
_____
_____

IN OTHERS' WORDS...

- "Nobody can make you feel inferior without your consent."

  —*Eleanor Roosevelt*

© 2007 Jones and Bartlett Publisher

SEXUAL HARASSMENT

- U.S.E.E.O.C. and harassment
  - Quid pro quo
  - Hostile environment
- Sexual harassment in schools
- Sexual harassment on campus
- Reactions to sexual harassment
- Sexual harassment in the military

© 2007 Jones and Bartlett Publisher

BIOLOGICAL FACTORS AND FORCIBLE SEXUAL BEHAVIORS

- Alcohol is a factor in 50% of rapes.
- Date-rape drugs produce disinhibition and amnesia-like effects.
- Younger people commit violent acts more often than older people.
- Women are hurt by men more often than men are hurt by women.

© 2007 Jones and Bartlett Publisher

PSYCHOLOGICAL FACTORS AND FORCIBLE SEXUAL BEHAVIORS

- Sexual abuse in childhood contributes significantly to the risk of development of mental disorders later in life.
- Adolescent rape survivors have more behavioral problems than older survivors.
- Women with low self-esteem tend not to end abusive relationships.

©2007 Jones and Bartlett Publisher

SOCIOCULTURAL FACTORS AND FORCIBLE SEXUAL BEHAVIORS

- Socioeconomic status plays a role; higher aggression found in lower income populations.
- People who believe in rape myths assign less blame to perpetrator, more to victim.
- Cultural belief in patriarchy—males dominant over females—can promote abusive behavior.

©2007 Jones and Bartlett Publisher

Chapter 16 Summary: Fill in the Blanks

Rape

Knowledge about forcible sexual behaviors has rapidly increased, but there is a great need for continued study. Many myths still exist about rape and other forcible acts. Those holding more traditional attitudes toward marriage assign more victim _____ than those with more egalitarian attitudes.

Rape is forcible sexual intercourse with a person who does not give _____. Statutory rape is intercourse with a person under the legal age of consent. Stranger rape is rape of a person by an unknown person. Acquaintance rape is rape by a friend, acquaintance, or a date—also known as date rape.

Theories vary about why people commit rape. Major characteristics of rapists often involve a desire for _____ over their victim rather than sexual pleasure; although, some researchers think sadistic rapists may be aroused in response to assault and violence. This occurs in a dating situation much more often than most people think, but many steps have recently been taken to deal with the problem. Rape survivors commonly experience symptoms such as dreams and nightmares, sleep disturbances, and impaired concentration. Help is usually needed to deal with the effects of rape.

There is increased recognition that males can also be rape survivors. Social responses to rape include establishing rape crisis centers, presenting courses dealing with rape prevention, improving methods of helping victims, and revising laws.

Pedophilia

Pedophilia denotes feelings of adult sexual attraction to _____, and the offender is usually a family friend, relative, or other acquaintance. There is an intergenerational pattern of child abuse, and victimization can lead to revictimization.

Incest

Incest is sexual behavior between relatives who are too closely related to be _____. Survivors of incest often believe it is their fault. The characteristics of offenders are similar to everyone else except for their incestuous desires. Various community organizations offer help for incest survivors and their families.

Spousal Abuse

Domestic violence relates to forcible sexual behavior and is a manifestation of intimate relationships. Battering is rarely a one-time event, and attacks usually increase in number and severity unless intervention occurs.

Sexual Harassment

Sexual harassment can include touching, verbal abuse, demanding certain sexual favors, or using threatening tones.

Harassment includes inappropriate verbal or physical conduct of a _____ nature. "In addition to being upsetting and distracting, workplace sexual harassment can be hazardous to health." Responses to sexual harassment can range from avoidance or defusion to negotiation or confrontation. A person being harassed generally has several options—personal actions, company grievance, union grievance (if applicable), and legal action.

Focus on the Facts

Use the following table to help organize your review of forcible sexual behavior contained in this chapter.

Researchers/Topics	Characteristics, findings, or statistics, and notes to help you remember.
Rape and Rape Myths p. 689	
Society and Rape p. 692–693	
The Rapist p. 692–693	
Date Rape *Ways to help* *Situational model* *Date-rape drugs* p. 693–702	
Incidence of Rape p. 702	

Researchers/Topics	Characteristics, findings, or statistics, and notes to help you remember.
Consequences of Rape Survivors Rape Trauma Syndrome p. 704–705	
Rape of Males p. 705–707	
Social Responses p. 707–708	
Pedophilia *Pedophiliac* *Incidence* *Effects* *Prevention* p. 708–717	
Incest p. 717–719	

Researchers/Topics	Characteristics, findings, or statistics, and notes to help you remember.

Spousal Abuse
   Marital rape
   Domestic violence
p. 719–726	

Sexual Harassment
   In schools
   On campus
   Reactions
p. 726–734	

Explain the Following Terms:

1. Rape:

2. Statutory rape:

3. Stranger rape:

4. Acquaintance rape:

5. Date-rape drugs:

6. Child sexual abuse:

7. Incest:

8. Sexual harassment:

Test Your Knowledge. Are the Following Statements True or False?

Page numbers are provided to help you check your answers as you study.

1. True   False   Most rapists rape to fulfill sexual urges. (p. 692)

2. True   False   The prevalence of dating violence is higher among black than white and Hispanic students (p. 693)

3. True   False   Rohypnol and GHB are two date rape drugs. (p. 701)

4. True   False   Someone is sexually assaulted every two and a half minutes in America. (p. 702)

5. True   False   Rape trauma syndrome may last several years. (p. 704)

6. True   False   Females can rape males. (p. 705)

7. True   False   Pedophilia is sexual behavior in which a child is the sexual object. (p. 708)

8. True   False   Child and adolescent sexual abuse increases the risk of teenage pregnancy. (p. 713)

9. True   False   A husband cannot be legally responsible for raping his own wife. (p. 720)

10. True   False   In some industrialized societies, domestic violence is considered to be nonexistent. (p. 721)

11. True   False   Sexual harassment includes verbal comments that create an intimidating or offensive work or school environment. (p. 726)

Activity 16.1: Changing Attitudes to Prevent Rape

Using what you have learned about how society and culture can influence sexuality attitudes and behaviors, suggest three ways that could be used to educate males and females about preventing date or acquaintance rape.

1.

2.

3.

Activity 16.2: WEBEX- What To Do If . . .

Go to the web to check out the Rape, Abuse & Incest National Network (RAINN) web site at *www.rainn.org/* or through the text web site below. Click on the link to "What Should I Do?" to provide a summary answer to the following questions:

What should I do if I am sexually assaulted?

How can I help a friend who has been sexually assaulted?

What can I do to reduce my risk of sexual assault?

You may not have children yet, but you may some day, or perhaps you have nieces/nephews you think about when answering the next question: *How can I protect my child from sexual abuse?*

Want to know more? You can find additional information about topics covered in this chapter at sexuality.jbpub.com.

Chapter 17: Sexual Consumerism

Learning Objectives

By the end of this chapter, you should be able to:

- Describe the ways in which sexuality is used in the mass media, including advertising, TV, movies, literature, popular music, and the Internet.

- Discuss what constitutes sexually explicit materials, the results of research on their effects, and efforts to control their distribution.

- Describe the different types of sex workers and the economics associated with sex work.

Chapter 17

SEXUAL CONSUMERISM

©2007 Jones and Bartlett Publishers

CHAPTER OBJECTIVES

- Describe the ways in which sexuality is used in the mass media, including advertising, TV, movies, literature, popular music, and the Internet.
- Discuss what constitutes sexually explicit materials, the results of research on their effects, and efforts to control their distribution.
- Describe the different types of sex workers and the economics associated with sex work.

©2007 Jones and Bartlett Publishers

MASS MEDIA AND THE ARTS

- Advertising
- Television advertising and programming
- Sexuality and the movies
- Videotapes, CDs, and DVDs

©2007 Jones and Bartlett Publishers

_____

_____

_____

_____

_____

_____

_____

_____

_____

_____

_____

_____

_____

_____

_____

_____

_____

_____

_____

_____

_____

_____

_____

_____

_____

_____

_____

_____

_____

_____

_____

_____

_____

_____

MASS MEDIA AND THE ARTS

- Literature
  - Books
  - Magazines
- Popular music
- Online material
  - Web sites and email
- X-rated computer games
- Sexual aids

© 2007 Jones and Bartlett Publishers

IN OTHERS' WORDS...

- "The difference between pornography and erotica is lighting."
  —*Gloria Leonard*

© 2007 Jones and Bartlett Publishers

SEXUALLY EXPLICIT MATERIALS: DEFINITIONS

- Obscenity
  - Personal or societal judgment that something is offensive
- Erotica
  - Sexually oriented material that may be artistically produced or motivated
- Child pornography
  - Use of minors in sexually explicit media

© 2007 Jones and Bartlett Publishers

CONTROL OF SEXUALLY EXPLICIT MATERIALS

- Legal penalties
- Civil rights and censorship
  - Pornography filters
  - Child Online Protection Act

©2007 Jones and Bartlett Publishers

IN OTHERS' WORDS...

- "I believe that sex is one of the most beautiful, natural, wholesome things that money can buy."
  —*Steve Martin*

©2007 Jones and Bartlett Publishers

SEX WORKERS

- Types of sex workers
  - Call girls, house prostitutes, street walkers, massage parlor sex workers, bar girls and strippers, male sex workers, pimps
- Opinions about sex work
- Controlling sex work
- The law and prostitution
- Child prostitution

©2007 Jones and Bartlett Publishers

BIOLOGICAL FACTORS AND SEX CONSUMERISM

- Prostitutes in general have higher rates of HIV.
- No externally used products can enlarge the penis or breasts.

©2007 Jones and Bartlett Publishers

PSYCHOLOGICAL FACTORS AND SEX CONSUMERISM

- Media images can negatively distort body image and self-esteem.
- Many ads use sexual imagery to attract attention and stimulate senses.

©2007 Jones and Bartlett Publishers

SOCIOCULTURAL FACTORS AND SEX CONSUMERISM

- Fraudulent sexual aids
- Prostitution outlawed in all but a few counties in Nevada.
- Other countries allow prostitution.
- Some countries ban any sexually explicit materials.
- Media fail to depict safer sex practices.

©2007 Jones and Bartlett Publishers

Chapter 17 Summary

Mass Media and the Arts

Sexual themes and products are big business; therefore, they are prevalent in magazine and newspaper advertising, television advertising and programming, movies, videotapes, literature, popular music, and online materials. Some people argue that sexual themes used to sell products unrelated to sexual activity is sexploitation, with the potential for sexism. They believe this practice will lead to women being viewed as sex objects, feelings of sexual inadequacy on the part of men and women, and unrealistic sexual performance demands. Some people believe that sexual commercialization is a healthy practice. They believe such a practice leads to greater sexual excitement and enjoyment, increased sexual knowledge, and a desensitization of people to the emotionally charged topic of sexuality. Differing perceptions of ads for condoms and sexual enhancers like Viagra, for example, indicate the impact that advertising can have in certain circumstances. (p. 743)

Advertisements appeal to sexual needs, leaving the impression that if one buys the product, the sexual needs will be fulfilled. These appeals are made to both males and females. Television has become highly eroticized, usually by innuendo or teasing. Many television series feature attractive men and women involved in sexual exploits to attract viewers. In fact, it was found that the sexual content of all TV shows was up 96% since 1998. (p. 748)

Cable television programs often are sexually explicit. Since cable is available only to those who buy access to it, some people feel that explicit sexual activity is appropriate for viewers who choose it. Consequently, cable companies have programmed shows and movies that would not be approved by regular network censors.

Sexual themes have been attractions in movies for a long time. However, in the 1960s and 1970s, sexual permissiveness and experimentation permeated the movies, as well as other segments of society. Today, sexually explicit movies are advertised side by side with classical music concerts, Broadway shows, and other more traditional forms of entertainment.

The videotape, CD, and DVD market for sexually explicit material has grown by leaps and bounds. There are many videotape, CD, and DVD rental shops where sexually explicit videocassettes can be rented and viewed in the home. In addition, web sites offer both still photographs and X-rated videos at every level of explicitness. Ten percent of the most visited sites on the Internet are sex-oriented. (p. 758) This trend has alarmed some people, who believe such behavior is immoral; whereas others view this trend as healthy, since it fosters sexual satisfaction and an openness about sex.

Sexually explicit literature is not a new phenomenon. There are many examples of early erotic literature. In addition to this type of literature, a how-to publishing business has developed to help people reach their sexual potentials.

Popular music has experienced an influx of blatant sexuality. Lyrics (words and grunts), performance (movement and costume), and provocative photos on album covers use sexual suggestion and appeals to our sexual fantasies to sell the music and the entertainer. Groups of citizens have banded together to attempt to ban sexually explicit music from the airwaves and have sometimes been successful. Online materials have given people of all ages access to sexually explicit pictures, stories, and other examples of "cyberporn."

Another aspect of sexual commercialization is selling the promise (and sometimes the reality) of more satisfying sexual activity through the use of sexual devices and other aids. Some of these products work as advertised, and others do not. In some localities, sexual boutiques have replaced "porno-sleaze" shops to sell sexual aids, and Tupperware-type parties make the selling and buying of sexual aids more acceptable.

Sexually Explicit Materials

National conservative and some national feminist groups have formed an uneasy alliance fighting the availability of sexually explicit materials that, in particular, depict women as sex objects or depict violence against women. Whether the motivation is one concerning the morality of depicting sexual topics altogether or with the degradation of women, or both, the "Porn War" is on.

Among the forms in which sexually explicit materials may be found are motion pictures, videotape cassettes, DVDs, magazines, cable television, Dial-A-Porn telephone services, and online sources. Two national commissions have studied pornography and have reported contrary findings. The Report of the Commission on Obscenity and Pornography in 1970 found pornography to be unrelated to sexual violence. The Final Report of the Attorney General's Commission on Pornography in 1985 found that "substantial exposure to sexually violent material bears a causal relationship to antisocial acts of sexual violence." In recent years there has been increasing concern about children being used in sexually explicit material (child pornography) and concern about continued eroticization of young children in the print media and on television.

Sex Workers

Prostitution refers to any situation in which one person pays another for sexual gratification. There are different types of sex workers: call girls (and boys), house sex workers, streetwalkers, massage parlor sex workers, and bar girls and strippers. Sex work is big business. More than one million people in the United States have worked as sex workers. Several methods have been tried to control sex work. These include the Control Model, the Regulation Model, and the Zoning Model. Each model has its advantages and its disadvantages.

A particularly disturbing feature of the sex work business is the presence of minors selling sexual activity. Child prostitution has become more common in recent years as the number of runaway children grows, and they attempt to independently care for their needs. Adolescent sex workers tend to have not completed high school, nor are they employed elsewhere.

Focus on the Facts

Use the following table to help organize your review of sexual consumerism as it is described in this chapter.

Researchers	Type of research, findings, or statistics, and notes to help you remember.
Advertising p. 742–745	
Television Advertising and Programming p. 745–750	

Researchers	Type of research, findings, or statistics, and notes to help you remember.
Sexuality and Movies; Videotapes p. 751–754	
Literature p. 754–755	
Popular Music; Online Material p. 755–760	
Sexual Aids p. 760–762	

Researchers	Type of research, findings, or statistics, and notes to help you remember.
Sexually Explicit Materials *Definitions* *Effects* p. 762–766	
Child Pornography p. 766–767	
Controlling Sexually Explicit Materials p. 767–770	
Sex Workers and Prostitution; Laws p. 770–781	

Fill in the Correct Terms to the Following Definitions:

1. Use of minors in sexually explicit media. _____

2. Highly paid female sex workers who work by appointment only. _____

3. Sex workers who work in brothels. _____

4. Sex workers who work on the streets. _____

5. Place where sex workers can be hired to perform sexual acts under the guise of giving a massage.

   _____

6. Sex workers who are supposed to act available so customers will buy them drinks. _____

7. A man who is paid to provide escort and sexual services, usually for wealthy, middle-aged women.

   _____

8. A male sex worker who performs homosexual acts for pay. _____

9. Individuals who set up female sex workers with clients. _____

Test Your Knowledge. Are the Following Statements True or False?

Page numbers are provided to help you check your answers as you study.

1. True   False   Television programming does not affect what teenagers know about sexuality (p. 746)

2. True   False   SHINE awards honor those in the entertainment industry who incorporate accurate and honest portrayals of sexuality in their programming. (p. 749)

3. True   False   Sexually explicit content in the media is a fairly new development (last 20 years). (throughout chapter)

4. True   False   When two or more people engage in simulated sex talk online, they are participating in cybersex. (p. 760)

5. True   False   Women can enhance their breast size by applying external products such as lotion. (p. 760)

6. True   False   At any given moment, there are approximately 20,000 sexual predators online. (p. 760)

7. True   False   Obscenity is a universally recognized judgment that something is offensive. (p. 762)

8. True   False   Sexually explicit materials may have some educational benefit. (p. 763; throughout chapter)

9. True   False   Prostitution involves participating in sexual activity for pay or profit. (p. 770)

10. True   False   Prostitution is illegal nearly everywhere in the United States. (p. 770)

Quick Questions:

After reading the chapter, explain the following:

What is the difference between erotica, pornography, and obscenity?

Who decides if a picture or work of literature is erotic, pornographic, or obscene? What criteria should be used to evaluate sexually explicit works?

What measures can you suggest to safeguard the Internet for children, while still allowing adults the freedom to view and explore sexually based web materials?

Activity 17.1: Pop-Culture Media Messages About Sex

After watching a movie or reading the lyrics of a song that relates to sexuality in a clear way, answer the following questions:

What movie/music did you select? (Title: actors, authors, composers)

Provide a short summary of what this medium is about:

How does the sexuality message in this medium relate to content covered in this course?

If you were making this film or song, what would you change to promote sexual health based on what you have learned from class and your text? If you would not change anything, give specific examples of how this film or song presents a message about healthy sexuality?

Activity 17.2: Media Analysis of Sex for Sale

Find and attach an article, cartoon, or advertisement that uses sex to sell you something. Analyze the medium's portrayal of sex as a marketing tool. Answer the following questions:

What is the message of sex and the product?

What examples are used to convey this message?

How do you think college-age individuals would respond to this message? Explain by gender:

Males   Females

Activity 7.3: 3-D The Price of Prostitution and Pornography

Prostitution and pornography have been part of our sexual culture for a long time and are not likely to go away, even if they are illegal where you live. The impact extends beyond two individuals exchanging goods for services. Whether or not you have ever bought or sold, we all pay for prostitution. Explain how the following dimensional factors can be tied to prostitution and pornography

Biological Factors and Prostitution/Pornography:

Psychological Factors and Prostitution/Pornography:

Sociocultural Factors and Prostitution/Pornography:

Want to know more? You can find additional information about topics covered in this chapter at sexuality.jbpub.com.

Learning Objectives

By the end of this chapter, you should be able to:

- Define *ethics, morals, ethical principles, ethical dilemmas, values,* and the five ethical principles that serve as a basis for deciding whether a decision is moral.

- State the ethical considerations of such sexually related topics as sexually transmitted infections, sexual activity between unmarried partners, sodomy, contraception, abortion, amniocentesis, fetal tissue implantation, prostitution, in vitro fertilization, genetic engineering, and sexual responsibility to a partner.

- Identify the rationale for laws pertaining to homosexuality, obscenity and pornography, rape, statutory rape, adultery, and divorce.

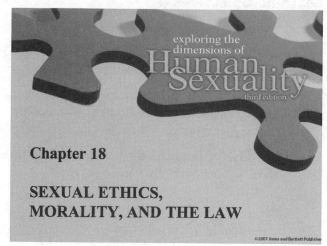

Chapter 18

SEXUAL ETHICS, MORALITY, AND THE LAW

©2007 Jones and Bartlett Publishers

CHAPTER OBJECTIVES

- Define *ethics, morals, ethical principles, ethical dilemmas, values*, and the five ethical principles that serve as a basis for deciding whether a decision is moral.

©2007 Jones and Bartlett Publishers

CHAPTER OBJECTIVES

- State the ethical considerations of such sexually related topics as sexually transmitted infections, sexual activity between unmarried partners, sodomy, contraception, abortion, amniocentesis, fetal tissue implantation, prostitution, in vitro fertilization, genetic engineering, and sexual responsibility to a partner.

©2007 Jones and Bartlett Publishers

CHAPTER OBJECTIVES

- Identify the rationale for laws pertaining to homosexuality, obscenity and pornography, rape, statutory rape, adultery, and divorce.

© 2007 Jones and Bartlett Publisher

ETHICS: THE BASES FOR MAKING DECISIONS

- Moral and immoral
- Ethical principles
  - Nonmaleficence (do no harm)
  - Beneficence (do good)
  - Autonomy/liberty (people should be free to make their own decisions)
  - Justice/fairness
  - Social utility (what is best for society)
- Ethical dilemmas

© 2007 Jones and Bartlett Publisher

MORAL DECISION MAKING AND SEXUAL BEHAVIOR

- Commonly accepted ethical principles
- Sexually transmitted infections
- Sexual activity between unmarried partners
- Sodomy

© 2007 Jones and Bartlett Publisher

MORAL DECISION MAKING AND SEXUAL BEHAVIOR

- Contraception
- Abortion
- Amniocentesis
- Fetal tissue implantation

©2007 Jones and Bartlett Publishers

MORAL DECISION MAKING AND SEXUAL BEHAVIOR

- Prostitution
- In vitro fertilization
- Genetic engineering
- Sexual responsibility to a partner

©2007 Jones and Bartlett Publishers

LAWS REGULATING SEXUAL BEHAVIOR

- Homosexual activity
- Obscenity and pornography
- Rape
- Statutory rape
- Adultery
- Divorce

©2007 Jones and Bartlett Publishers

Chapter 18 Summary: Fill in the Blanks

Ethics: The Basis for Making Decisions

Ethics is a system on which we base our moral decisions. Ethical principles provide guidelines for abstract questions, not solutions to individual cases. When ethical principles clash, we have an ethical dilemma. Sometimes religion or culture provides answers to ethical dilemmas. _____ ethics are principles intended to guide people with decision making in all situations. These principles are explicit, specific, and all encompassing.

_____ ethics are based on the premise that all situations are unique, and therefore no one set of rules is applicable in all cases. Morals relate to concrete decisions in particular situations. If the decision is consistent with our values, it is moral; if it is inconsistent with our values, it is _____.

Moral Decision Making and Sexual Behavior

If a decision or action is moral, it is "good" or "right." If it is immoral, it is "bad" or "wrong." Laws represent the encoding of generally accepted societal views of morality. When these views are not representative of a societal consensus of morality, they are not followed and often need to be changed.

Our laws regarding sexual behavior have developed from a general acceptance of specific ethical principles, values, and judgments about behavior. They have their roots in experience, in religious dogma, and in economics and politics.

Sodomy is a category of sexual behaviors defined as illegal by a state. Sodomy laws have been used to prosecute homosexual behavior (even if conducted in private) and have been used to prohibit particular heterosexual behavior (for example, anal intercourse). In response to the 1987 Supreme Court ruling that refused to protect private homosexual activity, groups have lobbied state legislatures to eliminate from the statutes sodomy laws preventing consensual sexual behavior between adults conducted in private. In 2003, the Supreme Court ruling was overturned. (p. 794)

The fear of AIDS has led to several ethical issues. Should limited research funds be devoted to finding a cure for people with AIDS, or should that money go into preventing HIV/AIDS in the first place?

Sexual morality is a consideration in such behaviors as sexual activity between unmarried partners; the use of contraception, abortion, and amniocentesis; and prostitution.

Laws Regulating Sexual Behavior

Laws related to homosexuality, obscenity, rape, adultery, and divorce are examples of institutionalized morality.

Focus on the Facts

Use the following table to help organize your review of the sexual ethics morality and laws highlighted in this chapter.

Topic	Type of research, findings, or statistics, and notes to help you remember.
Ethical Principle and Dilemmas p. 791–794	

Topic	Type of research, findings, or statistics, and notes to help you remember.
Moral Decision Making and Commonly Accepted Principles p. 794–795	
Ethics and STIs p. 796	
Ethics and Unmarried Partners p. 797–798	
Sodomy p. 799–806	
Ethics and *contraception, abortion, amniocentesis, fetal tissue, stem cells, prostitution, In vitro Fertilization, Genetic engineering* p. 806–807	

Topic	Type of research, findings, or statistics, and notes to help you remember.
Responsibility to a Partner p. 806–807	
Laws Regulating Sexual Behavior p. 807–811	

Explain the Following Five Ethical Principles As They Relate to Sexuality:

Nonmaleficence:

Beneficence:

Autonomy/Liberty:

Justice/Fairness:

Social Utility:

Explain the difference between situational ethics and rule ethics:

Match the Following Concepts to Their Appropriate Definitions As Described in Your Text

a. Ethics

b. Moral

c. Immoral

d. Ethical principles

e. Ethical dilemma

f. Rule ethics

g. Situation ethics

h. Sodomy

i. Obscenity

j. Pornography

k. No-fault divorce

l. Alimony

1. _____ A belief that no one set of rules can apply to all situations and each specific situation must be analyzed to determine which ethical principles are applicable.

2. _____ Money a divorced person is instructed by the courts to pay regularly to his/her ex-spouse.

3. _____ Specifically refers to anal intercourse, but is often used to refer to almost any sexual behavior someone might not consider normal.

4. _____ Sexually arousing music, art, literature, or films.

5. _____ When two or more ethical principles work in opposing fashion in a particular situation, resulting in bewilderment regarding what is moral and what is immoral.

6. _____ Guiding principles used in all situations to arrive at moral decisions, which are considered applicable to all situations.

7. _____ The granting of divorce without either partner's proving the other was the cause of the marital failure.

8. _____ What is judged to be wrong according to a system of ethics.

9. _____ Something offensive to modesty or decency, often sexually related.

10. _____ Guides by which we can judge an action or decision as moral or immoral.

11. _____ A system that uses ethical principles to make decisions about morality.

12. _____ What is judged to be right according to the system of ethics.

Activity 18.1: Sense of Right or Wrong?

Read the following ethical situations. Should situational or rule ethics be applied to each situation described? Write a brief statement to explain what you feel is the right thing. Explain why you feel that way.

A husband has an extramarital affair and his wife then contracts an STI from him. Should he have told her about the affair so she could have protected herself?

After a divorce, a couple argue over what to do with their frozen pre-embryo's from in vitro fertilization. She wants to have a baby with them. He refuses to pay child support, since the child was not born during their actual marriage.

College freshman Amy is 19 and pregnant. She is convinced she has no desire to share parenting with her ex-boyfriend who is abusive. Her parents have always said if she were to get pregnant they would no longer support her. Amy does not want to have a baby right now. She wants to complete her degree and go to medical school.

Activity 18.2: WEB-EX State Laws

SIECUS believes that it is important to look at the states' sexuality related laws in total rather than by a single issue. SIECUS has, therefore, compiled information on state laws on a variety of sexuality-related topics. Access the *SIECUS State Profiles (2004)* through the "Want to know more?" section on the text web site at *www.siecus.org/policy/states*

Look up the laws your home state has regarding sexuality issues.

What is your home state? _____

Are you surprised by any laws that are still "on the books" in your state regarding sexual issues?

What "Events of note" are presented for your state? Choose one event and write your reaction to it.

Choose another state. How do the sexuality laws in this state differ from those in your own state?

Want to know more? You can find additional information about topics covered in this chapter at sexuality.jbpub.com.